Title page

Ancient Harappans Speak!
After 5000 years

A linguistic breakthrough

Collection of nine articles

Author
V.P. (Ponmuthu) Shanmugham

Copyright Page

After 5000 years!

Title: Ancient Harappans Speak!
After 5000 years (90 pages)

A Linguistic Breakthrough

ISBN: 979-8-9940362-3-5 (Paperback)
ISBN 979-8-9940362-4-2 (eBooks)
ISBN: 979-8-9940362-2-8 (Hardcover)

Author's notes

This author's research work on Indus Valley Civilization (IVC) extents the current researches with an innovative approach and enables consistently reading more than 2800 seals as a language and obtain insights from these readings. This bilingual full research is published separately (ISBN: 979-8-9940362-6-6). This collection of articles (also published separately in the Tamil Language) summarizes the full research focusing on:

Uses of seals, Tamil Grammar, Worship, Governance, Farming, Animal Husbandry, Relationship between Seals, and Writing Styles of Indus-Harappan Script.

This is a <u>collection of nine articles</u> based on the research that explored the Indus-Harappan script as both spoken and written language. This hypothesis is proved beyond a reasonable doubt by identifying the vowels and consonants (total number under 30) used and the syllabic structure that enabled the Indus-

Harappan people to sound all the syllables of their already fully developed spoken language. This living language is now spoken by 80 million people in the globe. These nine articles explore limited set of studied seals under each of nine topics to authenticate the hypotheses.

Some seal scripts are taken from RMRL (Roja Murthiya Research Library – Chennai, Tamil Nadu, India) Web Research Tool, https://indusscript.in Seal numbers are from ASI concordance – by Iravatham Mahadevan, IM 77, details shown in the bibliography. Edited seal photographs as credited in the bibliography. Most of the seal scripts in this book are as designed by this author based on the ASI Concordance.

** Indicates seals read by late researcher Purnachandra Jeeva who was the first researcher of the Indus-Harappan script who established that the script is a language and it is an ancient form of Tamil understandable by most Tamil speakers of the world today, in 2020.

This paper's author was born in a small agricultural village near Coimbatore, Tamil Nadu (India), finished high school in the medium of Tamil Language before getting undergraduate education in Engineering. Moved to U.S.A for graduate studies in engineering and management, and after thirty-plus year career in research work and retirement, continuing research, published a book on The Holy Couplet in 2023. Currently engaged in researching the Indus-Harappan script.

Author submits this work for evaluation on merit and use by the active researchers, scholars and interested readers.

Author
V.P. (Ponmuthu) Shanmugham
Chicago

Other Books By this Author

1.TITLE: Indus Script Is a Language; *சிந்து வெளியின் மொழி* – **in English AND Tamil. Sowmi Printers, Saravanampatti, Kovai, India. This research report reads the signs and seals of the Harappan civilization as a language. It reads over 350 of the 400+ signs and integrates the seal readings without conflict to establish that the Harappan language is spoken by 80 million people today. (300 pages)**

ISBN 979-8-9940362-6-6 (Hardcover)
ISBN: 979-8-9940362-0-4 (Paperback)
All available from Amazon KDP, and Ingramspark.
2. The Harappans Speak! After 5000 years. A linguistic breakthrough (Summary of the research in English)

Collection of Nine Articles covering nearly 200 Indus seals and establishing that the Indus Script is a living Language spoken today by 80 million people world over. (90 pages)

ISBN 979-8-9940362-2-8 (Hardcover)
ISBN 979-8-9940362-3-5 (Paperback)
ISBN 979-8-9940362-4-2 (e-book)

3.சிந்து=ஆரப்பன் குரல் ஒலி!

மொழி ஆய்வில் ஒரு திருப்புமுனை (தமிழ்). Collection of Nine Articles establishing that the Indus Script is a living Language by analyzing few hundred seals and integrating their reading without conflict to create a fuller picture of this ancient first known urban civilization of the Indian subcontinent (134 pages).

ISBN 979-8-9940362-5-9 (Paperback- Tamil) These books are available as paperbacks and some as hardcover, and eBook, printed on demand from various popular book sellers like Amazon KDP and Ingramspark.

Author's Forward

The pivotal key for this research is found in the two readings of ancient Tamil Literature, one is the Holy Couplet, Thiru Kural, and the other is the ancient grammar treatise 'Tholkaappiyam' both having no verifiable place and time of origin, other than claims and consensus. Truth by claim and consensus, indeed!

The unique interpretation not seen widely, is that the spoken language developed before written script appeared and developed, a readily agreeable linguistic concept. This concept applied to the study of the Indus-Harappan Script enables understanding of the sounds behind the signs. About 350 of them are identified out of 400+, and listed in the main research work.

As an example, the common crow is known in Tamil as "kaakkaa", the same sound of the bird's familiar call. This name came first in the spoken language before it was scripted with

© V.P. (Ponmuthu) Shanmugham

Indus-Harappan Script, later in Tamizi Script, and eventually in current Tamil. [Indus-Harappan 大太太, Thamizi ✝✝✝, and Tamil காக்கா]. Though the script is changing, the sound stays intact and *ancient*.

This principle is explained in the forward to the Tamil version of this collection of articles, with few examples, all of these are again expounded in the body of the main research with English translations, though the grammar is hard to translate into English for a non-linguist writer and reader, an attempt is made below with few examples.

This pictogram stands for a leaf of Ficus Religiosa, the sound 'arasa', a reference to the king. This script develops by adding two additional sounds *Na* and *a* as shown:

E🌿U → 🌿→ 327. arasa *Na a* = *arasana*, meaning the king's, a possessive seen in few seals, meaning consistent.

This being a pictogram in *evolution*, the scribe modifies this still into a geometrical form, a desire seen in the general architecture of the civilization as buildings and streets layout.

324. Though the form changes, the sound remains the same *'king's'*, a possessive. There is an intermediate form of this that can be seen in some seals.

This is a pictogram of a bat (vavaal – Tamil) whose uniqueness is in 'grabbing' onto small branches of trees and cracks in cave walls and rest hanging. Though this is seen used in some seals, the scribe is not satisfied to convey the (related to) 'grabbing' idea, and a new sign is developed to provide the same meaning, moving away from the pictogram.

367. This reads as 'vavyava', close to the sound *bat* (Tamil-vavaal) in sounding, providing the same meaning. We see seals that describe using these signs – laws *related to butter, about the cow belonging to the temple*, etc.

245. This sign is sounded as 'idam' or 'ida' meaning place, as a grid fixes a place. This sign in particular is used to provide a grammar, indicating a possessive relationship.

2950. Here we have four signs repeating a consonant, *y*. The is read as 'four y' but in Tamil sounds as 'nay', [*na* standing for four (*nanku*)], which is close to 'ney' (நெய்), clarified butter There are many seals that provide such work around in the script to meet the sound of the developed spoken language.

Later on, we see the same meaning (nay = ney = நெய்) scribed as,

1133, 8031: Ψ||||, proving our hypothesis. There are few other seals similar in meaning.

1110. This seal reads as 'thava sa ma tha La thava N Na, in Tamil meaning an equipoised leader, not given to vagaries of human frailties, meaning a fit and qualified, revered leader. Such leaders' residence is referenced in the signboard at Dholavera.

thava NNa(l) arasana thava m tha r thava thava sa(m). The signs 4-7 conjugate according to Tamil grammar as 'thavathar', a qualified advisor to the king, adhering to the meaning of seal 1110. You may read the full study of the signboard later.

Even as the research key is obtained from the two ancient literatures mentioned, any researcher who approaches the study of the Indus-Harappan script with *inherent bias* (pre-conceived ideas on his own or accumulated by studying others ideas) will not find a lasting understanding. This is well demonstrated by the abundant results of this research for the past 100 years, mixed in with valuable research that bring out understanding showing fidelity to the field discoveries by equipoised researchers. This approach as demonstrated by harmoniously integrating all discoveries without conflicts is a valid approach to understanding this known first civilization of the Indian Subcontinent. Avoiding interjections of any and all divisions and diversions that formed well after the decline of this great civilization will help in bringing this multifaceted peaceful civilization that saw the 'World as A Big Home', from pre-history into history, and make the valuable lessons embedded within our reach.

Author
V.P. (Ponmuthu) Shanmugham
Chicago

Abstract

Indus-Harappan script has been known for over 100 years and in a continuing effort to understand this ancient script, a new approach is needed to break the stalemate. Such a breakthrough innovative attempt is this research.
The Indus-Harappan script is,

Not a code to be decoded
Not a cipher to be deciphered
Not an unknown language that needs a multilingual inscription key
Nor a cryptogram for decrypting
The Script IS that of a fully developed spoken language, spoken for a very long time.

The speakers of a well-developed language were attempting to create a *sound recording system* – for their day-to-day needs of a growing civilization

This evolved classical language is spoken today by 80 million people in over 150 countries worldwide

A spoken language must have existed for a long time *before* a civilization succeeded in creating a written script, a continuation of the pictorial representation of their ideas in the past as seen in archeological studies as cave paintings, graffiti marks on potsherds, and even sculpted messages as at Gobekli Tepe, linguists can agree.

This is the approach taken in these nine articles explaining the full research. Of the more than 400 Indus-Harappan signs catalogued by ASI (Archeological Survey of India), this approach reads *about* 350 of them as the unit <u>sounds</u> (phonemes) of this ancient language. Using these unit sounds this paper reads few hundred Seals, most in turn, each helping to read few to few dozens more seals. In Animal Husbandry alone: Cow >1400 seals; milk>44; ghee>24; manure >60; laws>120; zebu cattle >100; children's food>160; etc. 7 topics>1900 seals. And there are many more topics and many read seals in the research, leading to an *estimated* number of seals readable to 2500.

In this study all these meanings of seals are integrated into a whole without conflict or contradictions, helping to create a fuller picture of this ancient civilization that is more than 5,000 years old. This research lays the foundation for further work to read all the artifacts to attempt complete understanding of this multifaceted ancient, perhaps the first urban civilization known of the Indian Subcontinent, *perhaps* of the world of that time.

The main research lists over 350 of the 400+ <u>*signs*</u> listed by ASI Concordance, and these sounds (letters, syllables, compound letters, and words) are used to read few hundred <u>*seals*</u> in this research. This 'signs and their sounds' are detailed in the main research. A brief summary of this is given in Article 7, *Sound Modifiers*, and some may find it beneficial to read first.

Another note on the signs: this author's vocabulary is limited to his lifetime experiences in farming, animal husbandry, dealing with laws, and learned philosophy and worldview of Tamils in his growing up years, which has helped with identifying the 'basic sounds' (phonemes) of about 350 out of 400+ signs of the Indus-Harappan Script.

What is needed to complete this study is for researchers with background in pottery, weaving, metalwork, carpentry, ship building, sea voyage, etc., to come together and read the rest of the seals with given insights in this work, to arrive at a fuller picture of this ancient multifaceted first Indian Civilization.

*****

© V.P. (Ponmuthu) Shanmugham

Table of Contents

Article 1: How seals are related

ASI Seals: 2648, 4718, 1110, 2234, 1425, 2689, 2068

Seal 1: ASI No. 2648. Ghee Shed

Seal 2: ASI No. 4718. Oh my! Milk!

Seal 3: ASI No. 1110. Equanimity

Seal 4: ASI No. 2234. Brotherhood

Seal 5: ASI No. 1425. Elders' Home

Seal 6: ASI No. 2689. Mature cow

Seal 7: ASI No. 2068. Mother Tamil

2648 ⊞ Ψ ⅠⅠⅠⅠ'' ◇ = mee mee nay thozu = Very good ghee shed

Here we read this seal as a language with consistent sound values for each sign, pictograms, and tally marks in the main research paper, with identifiable grammar guidelines -

◇ = mee = Respectable

The sound of the 'diamond' shape is *m / ma*, a consonant *and* a syllable. The modifier ⌄ adds 'e' sound to it- reading it as *me / mee*, both short/long syllables. There are two other forms for this sound as it evolved. Stratigraphy data will provide the sequence of evolution not attempted in this research. Both forms are seen in seals carrying the same sound.

ⅠⅠ = The 'ditto' *like sign* requires the reader to double the sound(s) before it, in this *right to left* scribed seal. The meaning here is akin to 'very', an emphasis, as in *'very' respectable*. There are also single 'ditto' marks with different meaning, explained as it occurs, in studied seals.

ⅠⅠⅠⅠ = The tally mark for four (4) stands for one of two letters *na*, and *naa* (short and long) in the Tamil language. This is in line with sounds for tally mark, ⅠⅠⅠ *three,* that stands for *mu* and *muu* (மு & மூ) (short & long) Tamil letters with identical meaning [one, two, three, six, seven – all are similar]. Though the usage for three (and others shown) as *mu* and *muu* with same meaning is still in use in Tamil, the usage of *na* and *naa* (ந & நா) is no longer used the same way in Tamil. The letters have taken on differing meanings.

Ψ = This sign stands for both *iy* and *ya* (ய், ய) Tamil letters, one is a consonant and the second is a syllable, in the Indus-Harappan script. The combined sounding with *na* read before, is *'naiy'* (நய்) and *'naay'* which in Tamil *sounds* as ghee (ney=நெய்).

See 2950 Ψ Ψ ΨΨ = iyiyiyiy= 'na' y. A modifier might have clarified this sound as *'ney'* (நெய்) but the nascent state of development of Indus-Harappan writing was not there yet; they would have sounded it 'correctly' as they were speaking this already developed language not limited by the script. This concept of *modifiers* is seen evolving as seen and studied in other seals (See article 7). The modifiers are maturing in later Tamizi script, sometime they picky-back on each other to correctly *sound* 216 syllables, maturing to 21 unique modifiers in Tamil to sound all 216 *syllables with only one picky-backing modifier, linking Tamil to Tamizi days*. This provides one of the proofs for *Indus-Tamizi-Tamil* evolution. You will see others throughout the research. See article 7 on Sound Modifiers.

⊞ **=** This pictogram stands for *'cowshed'*, this plan- layout - is still used in the southern parts of Tamil Nadu, India. The long unobstructed section is for the moving, standing and resting animals and the two smaller sections are for water and fodder for these animals.

 From here on, the paper reads the seals with sound values assigned in the main paper without explanations.

Once we read this seal (2648) as *"very good ghee shed"* we can proceed to understand the implications conveyed. This seal implies that there are other sheds, for cows (2014), for oxen (2167), for aged animals (5119), for valued strain of (zebu) cattle (1336, 4033) etc., because the needs served by the sheds are *specific*. It also implies a need of sheds for productive cows and such sheds existed to serve the public's need in a city environment that has controlling ordinances about housing cows. All these are *verified* below, and many other seals studied in the research cited and in other articles.

2014  = aa thozu = Cow shed [*aa* is a one letter syllable, *and* word in Tamil, meaning cow]

1387 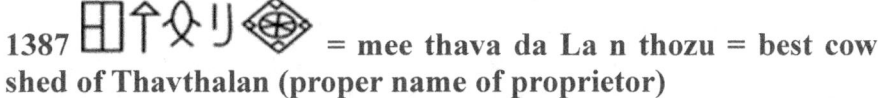 = mee thava da La n thozu = best cow shed of Thavthalan (proper name of proprietor)

1336 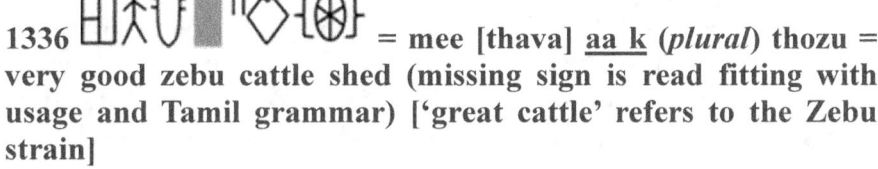 = mee [thava] <u>aa k</u> (*plural*) thozu = very good zebu cattle shed (missing sign is read fitting with usage and Tamil grammar) ['great cattle' refers to the Zebu strain]

2167 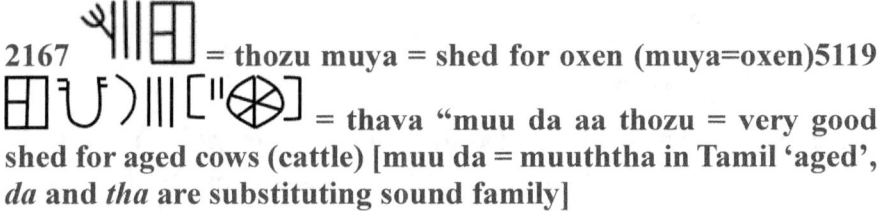 = thozu muya = shed for oxen (muya=oxen)5119 = thava "muu da aa thozu = very good shed for aged cows (cattle) [muu da = muuththa in Tamil 'aged', *da* and *tha* are substituting sound family]

Aquestion arises as to why a separate (2648) ghee shed? Here we gain insights into the social structure in terms of laws, ordinances specific to the city, products, quality control, food safety, people's activities and who created such laws and presence of any law enforcements.

Ghee shed implies that no milk was distributed there, like milk at a cow shed. We read many seals as shown below, involving distribution of milk, buttermilk, and ghee. These seals indicate that at the ghee shed milk was being converted to byproducts which were then distributed. Fresh milk being valuable we have to infer that it stays fresh for a limited time, before beginning to degrade, and there were existing laws that dictated that after a set time the distribution centers need to be closed and aging milk should be sent to the ghee shed *before* spoiling, for conversion to stabler, useful products like ghee. We also see seals as shown below, that state 'Kozi village guard', which stands for entirely different reason as 'Emergency Management Care Team' rather than as law enforcement. Studied seals reveal that the people were self-disciplined and study shows no seals so far in the research, that indicated the presence of external 'guards' to *enforce any* laws. We do have other seals studied to verify all these interpretations and related events:

4371 ᛃᚢ)ᚻᛩᛩᛟ = ma laa La paNNaa da aa Nai = order of the farmers guild [malaLa = gathered, grouped, collected, heaped] [paNNaa da = paNNadar= farmers] [aaNai – Tamil = command, order, law, ordinance] ['paNNaaddu (பண்ணாட்டு) is a Tamil word still in use.

3016 ᛏᛁᛁᛁᚢᛩᛩᚢᛋᛋ = di di ay laa iLa vya muu n = just expressed fresh milk

[de dee = 'thideer' –(திடீர்) Tamil = sudden, just now, instantly] [aila(sa) – Tamil, MalayaaLam = repeat action as moving an oar while boating, milking motion] [vya muu n = milk (derived studying over 15 seals; there are 44 seals with this syllable)]

1427 ᚢ ᛁᛁᛁᛁᚸ = kar na y = ghee seller [ney kar – Tamil, neykarar= ghee seller] [names of villages in Tamil Nadu – 'neykkaara patti'] Other signs 'kar', 'irkair','kaarar'.

2617 ᛁᛁᛈᛁ ᛁᛁᛁᚢᛩ'ᛝᛝ = vva da d l vya mur muraa = buttermilk available here [vva da d l -Tamil, ivvidaththil = here] [nur muraa-Tamil, MalayaaLam = muthu mor, muda mor = buttermilk] [single tally mark doubles the single sound before it, in this *seal*]

5274 ᛃᚢᚧᚏᚏ = ida ida ma [Tamil = of this place] aa Nai [Tamil = law] = ordinance of this place (village, city)

© V.P. (Ponmuthu) Shanmugham

8117 ᛤᎾ 🦢 = kozi (uur) aa Nai = Ordinance of Kozi (Village)

[wherever short and long 'u' sound was needed, the scribe inserted a picture or tally mark, as they did not separate out the long and short 'u' vowel signs to scribe; all tally marks and most pictures seen contain these 'u' sounds] This understanding is a major breakthrough, but simply put here and elaborated in the main study.

Seal 2: ASI catalogue no. 4718;

4718-line 1 ↑|||Ս|Ս|Ս Ψ Ս = ay ya ay o vya muu n [ஐயய்யோ -Tamil] = Oh my! Milk! = 'panic milk'.

4718 Line 2, |||Ս = a mu = ammu = toddler food [*ammu,* a toddler word still in use in Tamil and some Tamil family of languages. In 'amu' the middle 'm' doubles as 'ammu' a well-established scribing rule seen in many archeological findings related to Tamil culture]

This seal also consistently follows the sounding of signs as shown in the main research. The first 4 signs provide a *sense of alarm* (*Oh My God!*) and the last three *signs* combine to mean milk, hence "emergency or panic milk". The meaning is straight forward, the local ordinance stops milk distribution after a certain time (quality control on the freshness of milk). The aging milk, *before* spoilage is to be sent to the ghee shed for processing where milk cannot be distributed, only processed. People who need milk after-hours (sick, emergency workers, travelers, etc.) can still get milk at limited centers identified and *authorized* by this seal / imprint, for children's needs, with quality control on children's food. This in addition, indicates that these milk centers kept the aging milk simmering on low heat to preserve the freshness and it is safe for consumption. It goes without saying, that the ghee shed operated under an approved (2648) seal imprint from entrusted authorities!

Yet another conclusion we can draw, is that these (and all) centers interacting with the public, were setting up larger *notice panels* or banners with more details based on the authorization given by seal imprints, demonstrating one of the uses for the seals. Other articles explore many more uses of the seals and also in the main study. This further indicates the literacy rate of the people of the city or village being very high and writing/reading skills were not the exclusive domain of the elite and the 'powerful' as may be interpreted. This is also demonstrated by the graffiti marks seen on potsherds. Data democracy as practiced 5,000 years ago enabled by enlightened governance guided by equally enlightened advisors and level-headed leaders.

Seal 3: ASI catalogue no. 1110   Equanimity

ᛖᛖ⊕ᛩᚲᚳᚴ⊕ = thava sa ma tha La [Tamil- equipoised] thava N Na = thava NNal, = samathaLa thava aNNal [Tamil- அண்ணல் = leader] = Respected, equanimous, revered leader.

Here we have a description of a *'level-headed leader'* who is fit to be an advisor to the king or worthy of being a leader in the community who helps to create laws we see. This interpretation bears out when we see laws (in 128 other seals) to govern people's activities and is beneficial to all. This also implies that the leader or king is not dictatorial but an enlightened leader who is committed to strengthening the people from within and kept the need for governance to a minimum. And all this is done with self-disciplined advisors like this seal (1110) describes and identifies. There are seals studied that verify all these in the 9 articles, some of which can also be seen in the cited full research.

This is the most likely meaning of a part in the description seen in the DHOLAVIRA signboard we see below and read *left to right* as it is not a seal (Author's font design).

⊕⊤✿⊕◇╳│⊕⊕╳ **= thava Na arasana <u>thava m tha r</u> thava sa(m) = thava aNNal arasan's thavathar (and) thava sam = "Respected residence of king's <u>advisors</u> and grain store."

Seal 1110 provided the qualification of king's advisors, *thavam thar* (=thavathar- conjugation following Tamil grammar) seen in this sign board. In addition, we read 'grain store'. This does not convey that all grain production was stored and controlled here but only what is needed in an emergency, as we infer from the qualification of the leadership and other seals that provide safety for the city, not from ['vandals' and 'barbarians' as some researchers may interpret] intruders or "others" but as a helping, caring organization in emergency resulting from flood, crop damage etc. when the grain store acts as a buffer. It also indicates in this port city (?), that when grains were renewed during new harvest, excess grain was used in commerce – notably export overseas in sea trade with Sumerians / Mesopotamians and others.

One other underlying message is this: This signboard was put up by 'authority' and therefore does not need 'approval'. The inference is that if any signboard needs to be put up by an artisan or *'shop keeper'*, it needs approval via imprints of some seals, from enlightened, invested authority, again demonstrating one of the many uses of the seals.

4347 ⧣∪✿ = arasa aa Nai = dictate of the king
Overarching law issued by the king that may guide many other laws, like a 'constitution'.

3016 ⟨glyphs⟩ = di di aylaa iLa vyamuun = just expressed fresh (Tamil iLam= இளம்) milk (here) [seal / imprint authorizing distribution of fresh milk] and bound by local ordinances.

2503 ⟨glyphs⟩ = mee kozi (uur) kaaval = The great Kozi village (uur) security/care The seal shows an organized approach to securing the safety of the Kozi village in *times of need* (for care) – from disasters, crop failure, etc., and not from *'others'*.

Seal 4: ASI catalogue no. 2234; Universal brotherhood

⟨glyphs⟩ **= vay ya iru illam = vayya(m) [Tamil-world=வையம்] iru [Tamil – big] illam [Tamil- home=இல்லம்] = "The world is a big home."

Consistently (sounding) reading this seal as a language we encounter two modifiers. *Seal's* first two signs read as *'vai ya(m)'* with a silent suffix brought out, meaning the World. The tally mark for two also means big – likely the reason for tally mark's diminished size but not the 'ditto' mark seen earlier. The reading brings out a silent suffix, reading *'irum'* meaning big, verifiable in Tamil Literature.

The last is a word built on the *sound* 'il' (ல்/ல Tamil). The 'top hat' modifier stands for 'e' making the Tamil *syllable* 'il' (இல்); the second modifier of *four short lines* as shown, stands for one of four suffixes *(am, an, al, ar)* of which only one (sometimes more) fit the reading. Here the 'il' (இல்) gains the suffix *'am'*, resulting in sound *'illam'*, with the *'il'* sound doubling, a common grammar in Tamil scripts both ancient and modern till the very recent 'printing press' times, the word meaning Home. The seal reads as "The World is a Big Home" expressing universal brotherhood, a wisdom ripened over *perhaps* many *millennia* (cultural and linguistic antiquity) of this civilization, a sentiment much celebrated in Tamil literature to this day.

Now, see some seals related to temple leaders below.

1274 ⬒ = mee mee koyil N al/an = Highly respected temple leader. The modifier provides two suffixes that fit. The role of the temple leader (many shown temples) is further discussed in the main research paper.

2290 = mee mee koyil malai (na)dana yyaa = highly venerated dancing lord of the hill- temple (*aa* sign used as a modifier)

1708 = koyil ida NNaa aa = temple leader's cow (here *aa* can be either a modifier or single letter word, as *cow*, since temples received donated cows)

Seal 5: ASI catalogue no. 1425

= illam vya muu tha ni = vaya muu thani illam = The *seal* reading is "Home for the aged and alone"

This reading is consistent with the sound value assigned to each sign in the research *and* used so far. This seal shows the value placed in caring for the aged in the peaceful society all those millennia ago. We also see the same care extended to cows/oxen beyond their productive age. We see cowshed for the aged (5119) and carers of aged cows (3246, 8041) with needed 'certified' skills to care for them, all found in studied seals. This study and reading may raise more questions, naturally, about medicine, medical care, end-of-life rituals, etc., and need to be answered by studying the rest of the seals into an integrated understanding, that this study has demonstrated so far. See more examples below.

2097 U)|||⊞△ = koyil ida muu da aa = Aged cow of the temple [aged cow (cared for?) at the temple]

3246 ⋏U◯◯U⋨|||Ψ = vya muu La aa kaa vva = carer of aged cows [seal's leftmost five signs read as one sign: ⋈ 15] See details of script evolution in other articles.

5119 ⊞U)|||["⊗] = thava muu da aa thozu = very good cowshed for aged cows

Seal 6: ASI catalogue no. 2689

Line 1: U⋈⋎"⊗ = thava thava vaya sa aa = thava vaya sa aa = right aged (mature) cow

The seal reads as a 'very good age cow,' [not *very* aged but *right* aged] Scribing variation seen

Line 2: ⋔'⋉ = sa sa aar = sa sayaar = ready of age (to mate) to begin productive cycle

The seal reads as *ready of age* (to mate). Both line 1 and Line 2 of the seal *combine* to show a cow of age or maturity ready to mate and begin the cycle of productive life. Here the word *'sayar'* in Indus Tamil script is today's Tamil *'thayar'* (தயார்) erroneously attributed to Urdu, from Middle East, with whom (Sumerian, Mesopotamian) the Indus people traded merchandise and most conceivably cattle and shared the related vocabulary.

1127 𓂑𓏤 人 " 𐦀 = vi vi th kaavva = very good seed guard [may apply to seed stock, and stud (seed) bull]

Seal 7: ASI catalogue no. 2068

𝝠 U (𝖷) 𝕏 " ◇ 𝕏 ** = tha mi thami lza ththaL aa k = thami thamizaththaL aakkaL = 'Incomparable Tamil Mother's (temple) cows. The letter *tha* in the seal is scribed artistic to fit the name.

The last letter of this seal (as read from right to left) is *ka* or *ik* (க, கி), which stands for the suffix that indicates plural in Tamil. This seal expressing the sentiment of the ancient Tamils of Indus-Harappan civilization unequivocally that their spoken and written language is Tamil, understandable by today's Tamil speakers. Here we see Indus-Harappan people worshipping Tamil Mother, personified as a deity in a temple for her and have offered cows for its ongoing benefit. This puts to rest the question of the ancient language of the Indian Subcontinent and specifically the language spoken/written by the Indus-Harappan people, the root, the known beginning of the history of the Indian Subcontinent.

Conclusions

This brief treatise provides many insights into the Indus-Harappan civilization and its script that has remained mostly unknown for over the past 100 years from its discovery. Reading few of the seals as *Tamil language* (script & sound) we get insights as to how the seals were used and the language that was spoken and that of the script. It is *not a decoding, deciphering, nor a cryptogram to decrypt nor anything else to be broken, solved, cracked, or revealed* - but a spoken language fully developed and being spoken *with a rich oral literature*, and the written script was being developed (for the first time?) and evolving as the research shows.

The bilingual research is published as, சிந்து சமவெளியின் குறிகள் முந்துமொழியே, The Indus-Harappan Script is a language. ISBN: 979-8-9940362-6-6 (The ISBN declares this as written in Tamil, but it is bilingual- English and Tamil)

Article 2: Farming Life

Seals: 4371, 1035, 1045, 2459, 2614, 1447, 4430

ASI Seal 1: 4371- Order of Farmers Guild.

ASI Seal 2: 1035- Sivanna

ASI Seal 3: 1045- Guard of the field

ASI Seal 4: 2459- Farm Leader's Cow

ASI Seal 5: 2614- Shed for oxen

ASI Seal 6: 1447- Gathered Manure

ASI Seal 7:.4430- Order of Farm leader

ASI Seal 1: 4371

4371 **ⴹⵀ)Ⱈ⚹⚹Ⱄ** = ma laa La paNNa da aa Na =
malaaLa paaNNaada aaNai = Order of the farmers guild
[malaaLa = organized, gathered together]

This seal as rendered in Tamil language shows a process by
which farmers, a large vital group in this agrarian civilization,
created laws that are beneficial to all concerned. These laws are
many, concerning agricultural products, process, quality
control, safety of people and beneficial animals in all stages of
their lives. When we see laws from village leaders, the king, and
standing ordinances of a place (village), we infer that the laws
made by these Farmers Guilds, necessarily fit in with existing
laws for the benefit of the people – appropriate to their ideal of
"world is a big home" (seal no. 2234) expressed in worship
seals/imprints, *most likely* given at a temple during worship of
Tamil Mother (seal no.2068).

In this seal we see the farmers gathering as a group (malala =
organized, gathered, heaped, collected in a single place, etc.).
The outcome is 'aaNai' ⴹⵀ, an order, command, or law passed
presumably after level-headed discussions.

The laws governing the people were not dictatorial by a king or
a leader, but all groups of inhabitants under the guidance of a
king who in turn gets his advice from enlightened advisors as we
read (1110) elsewhere in our studies of the Indus-Harappan
Seals – some shown below:

4347 ⴹⵀ🍃 = arasa aa Nai = Dictate of the king [🍃 =
King's, as the sign evolved]

© V.P. (Ponmuthu) Shanmugham

4430 ⊟∪∪⊞ = paNNai yya aa Nai = order of the respected farmer

5274 ⊟∪⋈⊞⊞ = ida ida ma aa Nai = ordinance of this place (line 2 shown elsewhere: 'law' related to 'children's food')

2234 ⋔∥Ψ∪ = vayya iru illam = The world is a big home

2068 ⋏∪⊗⋏∥◇⋈ = thami thamilz ththaL aa k = incomparable Tamil Mother's (temple) cows. [⋈ - a beautified artistic version of the first sign]

Seal 2: ASI catalogue no. 1035

Ψ∥∥⊙"⋈ ** = si si vaN aaRu ya = SivaNNa aaRudaiya =Siva, leader, controller of the river

This seal describes one who has control over the river, an essential part of any agricultural endeavor, or a civilization for that matter. The name Siva may have a historical significance as read in many other seals.

The underlying facts are controlling a river for the benefit of agriculture and city use. The river being perennial fed by melting ice and snow in summer and added rain during other times with its highs and lows calling for damming and controlling the flow so as to be useful in all seasons, essentially water management, a hallmark of Tamil Society throughout its history.

2652 ⊕ ⊟ ⊙ ⋈ = si vaN paN thava = SivaNNa, the cultured

220 ∣ ⋈ ∣ = Sivam, Sivan = [Modifier gives *'am'* and *'an'* suffix to syllable *Si*. Two other suffixes, *'al'* and *'ar'* do not fit]

Seal 3: ASI catalogue no. 1045

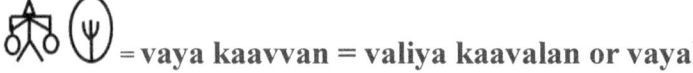 = vaya kaavvan = valiya kaavalan or vayal

Kavalan [⊌ ∣ = (Tamil)vayal = வயல்= cultivated field]

The seal reads as 'Strong Guard' or 'Field Guard', indicating a need for guarding the cultivated field. When we examine other related seals, this guarding is related to water management (enough water, too little or too much or no water at harvest) and guarding the field from perhaps wild animals. There is no question of 'guarding it from *others'* as may be interpreted

2503 = mee kozi kaavva = Gaurding / caring for Kozi Village [Kozi Village was guarded NOT from external threats but natural calamities. This is why Indus-Harappan people had a grain storage, for caring]

8041 = muu La aa kaavva = Guarding elder cows, the meaning of 'kaavva' (guarding) in the same light (caring) as in previous seal.

1447 = ma laa La saa Na = heaped manure [assembled, gathered, same meaning as in 4371]

1456 ⊟ ⋈ ⦀ ∪ ⟨⟩ ″ ◇ = mee "la vya muu sa Na = Very good aged manure

Above seals 1447, 1456 display an agrarian society living harmoniously, guarding the environment and fertility of the soil.

Seal 4: ASI catalogue no. 2459 with a missing sign filled

2459 ∪ ∪ ▨ ⚥ {⚕} = vaya Laar yyaa aa = vayal Lar yyaa cow = The respected farm leader's cow [can also be read as farm leader with the last sign as a modifier]

The seal with a missing sign filled-in, fitting with Tamil grammar reads Respected Field Leader's cow. The last sign (sound) is sometimes used as a modifier of the preceding sign, making it a long sound, which in this reading fits, meaning *respected field leader* and not his cow. In certain seals the later meaning may well fit.

This indicates the nascent state of modifier use in the Indus-Harappan Tamil script, which improves considerably in Tamizi where we can sound all Tamizi's 216 syllables and the development of modifiers fully matures in Tamil as 21 modifiers to sound all 216 Tamil syllables, unifying both Tamizi and Tamil syllabic structures. There are many seals with such inferences:

1098 ∪ ∪ ⟨⟩ ″ ◇ = mee " iLa yyaa aa = Cow of the respected young leader (the last sound can also be a modifier)

4084 ∪ ⋇ ⚥ ∪ ∪)⦀ = muu da av ay laa kai aa = cow of the elder lady. Here meaning is explicit as cow.

We see many seals of this type that can show ownership of cattle, the king to common citizen.

Seal 5: ASI catalogue no. 2614

⅄‖⊞ = thozu muuya = muuya thozu = Shed for the oxen (muuya=oxen)

The seal reads as "Shed for the Oxen", oxen being a very important draft animal in the early farming civilization and needs special care, different from other cattle, like cows, aged cattle and calves. The differentiation is in their feed, say cotton seeds, sesamum cake leftover after the extraction of oil. All of these are or may be covered by other seals.

2127 ⅄‖‖ eN y =எண் (எள்) ய்= எண் ய்= எண்ணை= eNNai= sesame oil; leftover is sesamum cake, in seals yet to be read.

1386 ⊞⋏∪▓"◇{⊕} = mee "aak thozu = Shed for Great cattle (Zebu) [Special focused care for zebu cattle]

1534 ⊞⋔⋇⋇"⧆ = muupa laa La n thozu = Cow shed of MuupalaaLan [Most likely a special shed, perhaps for milk *producing* cows]

2648 ⊞⅄‖‖"◇ = mee " ney thozu = very good ghee shed [a specialty shed for ghee production]

5119 ⊞∪)‖‖["⊕] = thava " muu da aa thozu = very good shed for aged cattle [Special care for aged cattle by trained carers]

© V.P. (Ponmuthu) Shanmugham

Seal 6: ASI catalogue no. 1447

⊟ ⋉ ⋔⋔ ⊂⊂ = ma laa La saa Na(m) = malaaLa saaNam (The meaning of 'malala' in 4371 verifies as gathered)= gathered, heaped manure

Here we have an important seal that connects cow sheds, sanitation of the cowsheds, farming, and guarding the fertility of the agricultural fields and duties of *'cowcarers'*. This seal declares that 'heaped manure' is available, most likely by a cowshed (not a ghee shed) for farmers to take to the compost pile or to the field if it is sufficiently aged. We have over 60 seals on this topic that fits harmoniously with practices in farming even now. All this verifies the mature civilization living in harmony with its environment likely guided by enlightened leadership and farmers.

4022 = mee mee vana iLa la saa Na tha ni = Very good field fresh cow manure, alone [The manure is declared as unmixed]

1350 = iLa la saa Na N = Fresh manure (available) [Scribe's attempt to declare fresh manure as available] Differing spelling by scribe.

1456 = mee mee la vaya muu sa Na = Very good aged manure (available), aged manure as more valuable, ready to use in the field. Different, but most common (correct?) spelling for manure.

The farmers may have created binding orders in handling manure from cow sheds. Cattle are not kept within the city boundary by laws or city ordinances.

Seal 7: ASI catalogue no.4430

ЕᲣᲣ⊟ = paNNai yyaa aa Nai = "order of the Farm Leader"

The seal indicates individuals can also issue orders, perhaps less broad in scope as opposed to laws passed by a farmers guild, as we read in seal no. 4371.

Conclusions: Article 2

The few seals we read as Tamil Language under the topic have shown some aspects of the farming life in the Indus-Harappan civilization. Farm owners, owners guild, their methods of creating orders, laws, their water management, managing the draft animals, guarding the field, its fertility and being a well-respected part of the population.

The seals we explored as Seven Seal on Farming Life in the Indus-Harappan civilization again demonstrate the relationship of people's way of life nearly five millennia ago closely matching the history of farming in the greater Tamil Land. Additional seals shown verify these conclusions. It verifies that the Indus-Harappan language, both spoken and written is Tamil beyond any reasonable doubt.

*****

© V.P. (Ponmuthu) Shanmugham

Article 3: Animal husbandry

Seals; 1339,1386, 2908, 4084, 3216, 5119, 1425

ASI Seal 1: 1339; Three Great Zebu cattle

ASI Seal 2: 1386; Great Zebu shed

ASI Seal 3: 2908; King's young cows

ASI Seal 4: 4084; Elder lady's cow

ASI Seal 5:3216; Carer of aged cows

ASI Seal 6: 5119; Shed for Aged cows

ASI Seal 7: 1425; House for elders

Seal 1: ASI catalogue no. 1339. Photo credit: Asko Parpola et all, Helsinki

1339 ⋃🗙🗙⦿||| = muu thava kai aa = Three great (Zebu) hand-raised cattle

This is an important seal that connects the Indus-Harappan culture to that of the current Tamil culture, by their admiration of this strain of cattle that is well adopted to the environment they live(d) in. See other seals below.

1407 ⋃🗙Ψ⊕ = thava N(Na) kai aa = Respected leader's hand-raised cow

1116 E⋃🗙🗙||| = muu thava <u>kai</u> aa Nai = Order from the elder sage

[Here the meaning is specifically the ownership (kai - possessive) for the order issued by a sage]

1028 ⋃🗙🐾⦿| = O vaN Lar kai aa = OvaNNalaar's cow
[Both the meanings of ownership and hand-raised cow fit]

[OvaNNal is a name found in the Sumerian clay tablets, where Sumerians elaborately describe this leader who came by ship, and taught them many details of building a civilization – buildings, farming, land measurement, creating laws, _writing_ etc. –explored in the larger study]

Seal 2: ASI catalogue no. 1386

A seal with a missing sign

1386 ⊞↑∪▮"◇⊕ = mee mee [thava] aak thozu = 'Cow shed for great (Zebu) cattle.' Here the missing sign is fittingly filled-in according to the study so far and Tamil grammar.

Here we see the special care and attention given to this strain of cattle demonstrating the value the *Indus Tamils* placed on this environmentally well adapted cattle line, a lineage most likely coming from *their* ancestors. Also, there are about 100 seals with reference to this type of hand-raised cattle and milk, demonstrating again the high value placed on this strain of cattle. The game of 'Jallikattu' about which there are seals, helped culturally preserve this strain by selecting breeding stock of this environmentally adapted strain and integrating the process with the brave lifestyle of Tamils of yesteryears and today. See a seal 4033, dealing with Zebu cattle:

Seal 3: ASI catalogue no. 2908.

2908 ∪❀ 𝚲 |||| = eezu njaan arasana aa = This seal reads: 'Seven young cows of the king.' [*young* qualifies the cow]

See; 2608 ∪❀𝖷 = iLa arasana aa = cow of young king. Later see seals describing just as the king, an elder lady has a hand-cared-for cow, likely a producing cow for her needs.

Here we see a seal declaring seven young cows belonging to the king. This matches with studied seals of cow carers who are authorized to care for cows of the king. There are seals showing cows and cow carers for cattle of everyday people as well (next Seal 4 studied: 4084).

2472 ❀∪❀ = arasa aa kaavvan = carer of king's cows [The king had cows and carers for them]

2514 ⚘||| = muu aakaavva = carer of three cows [seal permits cow carers and accounts compensation for his labor also]

4029 ⚘Ⓨ = vaya aakaavva = strong cow carer [cow carers are validated on skills]

We see seals for calves, older cows, coming of age cows, etc. in this study.

3328 ᛁᚱ∪⟩|||∪ = vaya muu dda aa oor = *an* aged cow [The last mark specifies the word (cow) to be singular, shown as number but not the sounds *o, oo,* or *ir*]

2689 ∪⧖ẙ"⊕ = thava "vaya <u>sa</u> aa = Right (mature) age cow [cow ready for breeding] [variation in scribing 'sa']

Seal 4: ASI catalogue no.4084

∪ ⚗⚘∪ ⒲⟩||| = muu da av ay laa kay aa = muuththa avvayin kaippasu = Elder lady's hand-raised cow = Hand-raised cow of the elder lady

As much as the king had cows, so also an elder lady was hand-raising a cow, most likely a milk cow, for her needs, and other seals also show cow carers who care for such cows as ones, twos and all the way to 7,9, and 3 times 12 cows and calves! (various seals)

This demonstrates the distance from the king and the people is minimal, indicating the enlightened governance and well-disciplined population with inner guidance needing no/minimal external enforcement. There are also seals, necessarily of baked clay and metal, that a cowshed gave out to owners of cows, establishing ownership to cow, calf and milk service rights.

2068 ⟨symbols⟩** = tha mee " thamiza ddaL aa k = Incomparable Tamil Mother's (temple) cows [Here we see cows offered to a temple for 'Tamil Mother' (Tamil personified)] ⟨symbol⟩ - Beautified artistic first letter on account of the subject, as shown in the seal

1561 ⟨symbols⟩ = koyil malay aa = cow of the hill temple [Temples owned cows as they were donated for the temples' ongoing benefits]

[seal examples providing deeper meaning of examined seal, and validate the study]

Seal 5: ASI catalogue no.3216

3216 ⟨symbols⟩ = vaya muu La vva aa ka = vaya muuLa <u>aakaavva</u> = Care(r) of aged cows (cattle) = ⟨symbols⟩ (same as 8041)

This seal shows an evolving script where five signs are integrated into one sign (word) by an innovative scribe to be efficient in scribing a seal where each line has labor content and the seal area is very limited. We see the last (as this is a seal) five signs combined into one sign, a word, ⟨symbol⟩, aa kaa vva, carer of cow(s). Here the last sound *aa*, is treated as a sound modifier integrating with *ka*, which method is also seen in many other seals, read appropriately. But the meaning of this seal is straight forward, "A carer of aged cattle" in four signs – and this speaks volumes of the lifestyle of the ancient Tamils of the Indus-Harappan civilization.

1228 ⚏🐦"◇ = mee mee koozi aakaavva = Cow carer of the great Kozi village

1030 ⚏|'↑|||∪ =vaya muu n oor aagaavva = carer of *a* milk cow.

2056 ∪∪↑)⊟"⊗ = thava " nadana ay<u>yaa</u> = Great dancing Leader

The last letter of the seal is used as a modifier.

Seal 6: ASI catalogue no.5119

5119 line 1 & 2 ⊞∪)|||["⊗] = muu da aa thozu = muu da aa thozu thava thava= Very good cowshed for aged cattle (cow).

In this seal the adjective "very good" is used for the cowshed and not as 'well aged' cattle, and hence two lines.

The meaning conveyed integrates with the previous seal (3216) of cow carer for aged cows. Both the seals clearly indicate the care and respect ancient Tamil showed for the aged cattle which is no longer productive, whether oxen or cow. Some seals with related reading shown below:

4084 ∪⚏⚏∪∪)||| = muu da av ay laa kai aa = Cow of the <u>elder</u> lady

8041 ⚏∪⚸||| = muu La aa kaavva = Carer of <u>aged</u> cows

2097 ∪)|||⊞△ = koil ida muu da aa = <u>aged</u> cow of the temple   [4084, 2097 : same signs for 'aged']

1456 ⊨⋈⫿⫿⫾⋃𝘅⫿⫿◇ = mee " la vya muu sa Na = Very good <u>aged</u> manure [8041, 1456 differ in signs to mean 'aged']

In these seals we see slight variations of scribing for the same meaning.

Seal 7: ASI catalogue no.1425

Ƴ𝝠⫿⫿⫿⋃⸱𝘅⸱ = illam vaya muu tha ni = vaya(thu) muu(ththa) thani(yor) illam= home for the <u>aged</u> and alone. This meaning can be arrived at without the missing suffixes shown.

We can see the parallels in the civilization in caring for the aged, human or otherwise, five millennia ago. This may raise more questions of medicine and related practices that need to be explored in other seals.

A multifaceted civilization that has integrated all activities around a central value of "the world is a big home!" (seal 2234 as read by Mr. Purnachandra Jeeva and expanded by this author elsewhere) All syllabic sounds established by the research are used consistently to read all the seals with variation noted between scribes spread across one million square kilometers over 1800 years!

Conclusions: In this short treatise we were able to read seals as Tamil language with the same consistency for sounding the individual signs shown in the main research paper. This study reveals a sampling of the activities related to animal husbandry in this ancient Tamil civilization which has parallels in Tamils' life today world over.

*****

Article 4: Governance

ASI Seals; 4371, 5274, 4430, 4454, 8117, 1116, 4347.

Seal 1: 4371; *Order* **of Farmers Guild**

Seal 2, line 1: 5274; Existing Law

Seal 3: 4430; Order of Farm Lead

Seal 4: 4454; Leader's butter related order

Seal 5: 8117; Kozi (uur) aa Nai; Ordinance of Koli (village)

Seal 6: 1116; Order by Holy Elder

Seal 7: 4347; King's Dictate

Seal 1: 4371 ⟨glyphs⟩ = ma laa La panna da aa Nai
= Order by the Farmers Guild. (Panna da can be ⟨glyph⟩, sign not seen in ASI Concordance) [Tamil –paNNattu]

This seal uses a word "malaaLa" which is used elsewhere with the meaning of 'collected, organized, heaped, etc.' indicating the Tamil reading shown with its English meaning translated. The research indicates organized activities of farmers in this mostly agrarian civilization. The farmers' guild assembled and created laws presumably after deliberations that are beneficial to all concerned and that order fits within the existing *ordinances of the place* and *other laws* by *respected leaders* of the community and the *dictates of the king* who in turn is guided by *level-headed advisors (1110)*. All of these ideas are confirmed by seals studied, some discussed in depth in other articles, and all of them and some, studied in the research work mentioned earlier. Here the dictates of the king equal the constitution in statecraft.

4056 ⟨glyphs⟩ = tha da ma laa La n = Strong organizer. In this reading the meaning of 'malaaLa' is identical to the studied seal, 4371.

1447 ⟨glyphs⟩ = ma laa La saa Na = Heaped manure. Here again the meaning of 'malaLa' verifies with seals 4056 and 4371.

2059 ⟨glyphs⟩ = very good manure. There are more than 60 seals covering this subject, in an agrarian society that lived harmoniously with its environment, that addressed the sanitation of the cowsheds and safeguarding the fertility of the cultivated field and duties of a cow carer.

2061 ⊏ ⚹ ⨆ = aamu kaN Na = Respected Bull Faced Lord. The value the people placed on the subject is seen in worship of a deity.

1110 ⊏⊏⊕⋀⋂⋈⊕ = thava sa ma tha La thava NNa = respected equanimous, level-headed, great leader

4347 ⊏⨆🍃 = arasa aa Nai = dictate of the king [dictate in the sense of a constitution in statecraft]

8117 ⊏⨆ 🐦 = Kozi (uur) aa Nai = ordinance of Kozi village

Seals 4347 and 8117 show two existing laws. One is the dictate of the King and the other existing law of a place, the village. So, the orders of the farmers' guild we studied has to fit with these harmoniously.

Seal 2, line 1: 5274

⊏⨆ ▷⊞⊞ = ida ida ma aa Nai = Existing law of this place (village, city)

Seal 2, line 2: 5274 ⨆‖‖ = mu a = ammu = Children's food [The seal implies a 'law regarding *ammu*']

We read this seal in Tamil as 'prevailing law of this place' that is related to 'children's food'. In researching other seals connected (e.g. 'Ghee Shed') we can connect many of the activities of the community guided by laws created by groups or individuals responsible for the wellbeing of the people. These connections are explored in other articles in this series and all are explored in depth in the research work referenced earlier.

© V.P. (Ponmuthu) Shanmugham

There are about 128 seals covering the subject of 'aa Nai', or Orders/ laws/ dictates/ declarations or ordinances. We may not know detail of any of them because of the medium of writing. But this research indicates how they *may have* been created, by what authority, and what effect they had on the people. From the sense of a peaceful society, we have to infer that all laws were created for the benefit of the people, who themselves were living with ideals such as 'the world is a big home', an expression of universal brotherhood.

2234 = vayya iru illam = World is a big home.

Seal 3: 4430 = paNNai yya aa Nai = Order of the respected Farm Leader

Tamil reading of this seal is 'Order of the respected Farm Leader', indicating not only a Farmers' Guild creates orders by dialogue, respected individual Farm Leader can also issue orders, perhaps, applicable to a smaller domain of activity. Though we have many seals about 'orders' (128 seals) we may not know or read what those orders were in details. These may have been written out on media that may not have survived the ravages of time. Finding proofs will be next to impossible unless written on semi stable medium. But we deduce from other seals as to how they might have related to each other by context, which this research has attempted.

Seal 4: 4454

side 1: = mee aar tha = of the respected one

side 2: = (Na)N(Na) vavyava aa Nai = Order related to butter

Tamil language reading of this seal, sides 1 and 2 combined, sound as 'respected leader's order related to butter'. This reading is without conflict with the readings of many other seals which are explored in depth in the research paper mentioned earlier.

Seal 5: 8117 ꓱꓴ 𓅞 = Kozi (uur) aa Nai = (prevailing) law of Kozi (Village).

In reading this seal as Tamil, we encounter two subtilities of Tamil grammar and Tamil place names. Kozi is name of villages even now (one in Kerala State - Kozikodu, and another in Tamil Nadu – Uraiyur's former name). So, this connection to place names in Indus and Southern India is verifiable.

Another refined meaning for the pictogram, as the research explained in other articles (and in the book in detail) is that lacking short and long form of the vowel 'u' the Indus-Harappan script (scribes) used pictures to derive this sound. Of the more than 20 pictograms, except few (unfinished research) , all of them sound these two letters (u and uu) (sounds) in reading them as Tamil (உ , ஊ) . Here, in this seal (8117) we insert the word 'village' (ஊர்) as the name with long 'u' sound (uur) *implied* as it cannot be written but sounded in syllabic reading. Same applies to tally marks as <u>all</u> tally marks contain 'u' sound.

Seal 6: 1116 ꓱꓴꝏ⚺||| = muu thava kai aa Nai = Order of the holy elder

In this seal tally mark for three stands for 'muuththa' meaning elder. The next sign most likely started as a pictogram and became a sign, means *'thava'* a penance filled one. The compound letter next sounds as *'kai' (க ய்)*, in Tamil means *'kaiththu'*, a possessive *'udaiya'* (உடைய) in Tamil, close in meaning to *'s*, a possessive. The last two letters as a syllable sound as 'aaNai', or order (command, dictate, law, etc.). Hence the reading *'Order of the holy elder'*, showing the place of holy men in the society.

Seal 7: 4347 ⧉ = arasa aaNai = King's dictate.

This seal reads in Tamil as *'arasa aa Nai'*, Order of the king. Here again we see a pictogram, a Ficus (religiosa) leaf known in Tamil as 'arasa ilai'. We see again that the sound 'u' (short) is needed to sound 'arasu' (அரசுடைய) and pictogram is used to imply that sound. In long term usage the 'u' sound is unused and 'arasa' has been in common usage since IVC time. There are many seals with this pictogram also, with modifications with letter signs, one of the seven writing styles identified in the research.

Conclusions

In this brief discourse we studied seven Indus-Harappan seals related to law and governance. We see who were creating the laws for the benefit of the people and how they are created. We see existing laws that guide the creation of new laws so the intentions of laws are preserved. Laws, orders, dictates by Farmers Guild, Respected Farmer, Holy Elder, The King aided by his level-headed advisors all are guided by existing law of a place that serves the people. In this study we also see how Tamil grammar plays a vital role in the script and explained some of the seven writing styles used by the Indus-Harappan Scribes.

All of these studies verifying the hypotheses we started with, namely the Indus-Harappan spoken and written language and script are indeed Tamil, spoken today by 80 million people in more than 150 countries throughout the world.

*****

Article 5: Worship

ASI Seals; 2420, 1182, 2442, 1070, 2069, 2056, 2068

Seal 1: 2420; Compassionate Siva

Seal 2: 1182; Triple Eyed Lord

Seal 3: 2442; Five faced Lord

Seal 4: 1070; Lord Nandi

Seal 5: 2069; Salutation to the Sun

Seal 6: 2056; Great Dancing Lord

Seal 7: 2068; Peerless Tamil Mother

Seal 1: 2420 ⟨symbols⟩ = aaL av ee sa kar = Compassionate Siva (Imprint)

This seal described as ancient form of Siva described in the year1928 by Sir John Marshall after he introduced this ancient civilization as pre-Ariyan and pre-Vedic in 1924. This reading of the seal as a language bears this meaning he intuited: *Compassionate Siva.*

Tamils of Indus worshipped benevolent Siva in his yogic posture nearly 5000 years ago, a continuation from *ages before, we can surmise.*

Seal 2: 1182 ⟨symbols⟩ = kaN ay koyil eramba = The buffalo of the temple of the three eyed lord (imprint)

In this 'seal' we see Siva described as the Three Eyed, indicating His eye of wisdom. This is an *imprint* as it reads 'correctly' from left to right. The reason for the last syllable, a pictogram of an ant, which is a *homonym* for buffalo in Tamil. The reason for using a pictogram is that the script lacked short and long form of vowel 'u', which is needed for writing both the names (ant and buffalo), but the sound existed in the spoken form and this type of usage is seen almost throughout the writing in Indus-Harappan scripts verifying that the spoken language was well developed before writing began and developed.

Seal 3: 2442 ⟨symbols⟩ = da ay yi muka r = thada ayyi mukar = Strong Five Faced Lord (Siva as in seal 2420)

This seal again denotes Siva as the seal 2420 did, as we see three faces shown in seal 2420, implying two more faces, one on the back and one upward facing. This reading in Tamil brings readings of these two seals without conflict.

Seal 4: 1070 ⟨symbols⟩ = aamu kama N = The bull faced leader

This reading is a fitting name for a deity in an agrarian society. The same idea is repeated with slight variation to signs in other seals (2061 ᐸ ⚹ ᵁ– aamu kaN Naa = ஆமுகண்ணா). These variations demonstrate that of the many scribing centers (50?) creating the seals, the scribing was not uniform or consistent in utilizing the signs in creating, innovating, the seals and variations *within reason (rules of grammar) are expected*. See some more examples:

2648 ⊞⏚Ψ‖‖‖"◇ = mee mee nanku y thozu = very good ghee shed [na y = 'ney' (Tamil) ghee] [pictogram is 'shed']

2950 ΨΨ ΨΨ = 'nanku' (4) y = na y= ghee

2322 ⚘ΨΨΨΨ = aagaavva nanku y = aagaavva nay = Ghee by cow carer (all seals show differing signs)

The three seals above show variation by scribe(s) naming ghee. In Tamil language numbers one, two, three, six, and seven show similar behavior. Short and long form of their names mean same number/word. In the similar way Indus-Harappan scribes used the short 'na' and long 'naa' [த, தா] to mean the same number/word. Whereas all the shown numbers retained this property, name and number four ('na' and 'naa') have taken on differing meanings now.

Seal 5: 2069 ⋉ᵁⵗᵀⵑ⊕⊙⊕✴⊕ = 'thava thava' 'thava vaN thava' 'O Naa L aa Thapa' = Salutations to the Sun

This seal reads as adoration to the daystar, the Sun, indicating the Tamils worshipped the sun as source of all life, especially in their heavily agrarian civilization, which worship continues to this day among Tamil people.

Dholavira sign board:  **= thava NNa arasana thava m tha r thava sa (m) = Revered Leader the King's respected advisors (residence) and grain store. Even as the Indus-Harappan people worshipped the life-giving sun with so much reverence, they show the same reverence in naming the place of residence of the King's revered advisors and the grain store. The grain store as we analyzed elsewhere, was to meet the emergency needs of people during crop damage or failure or other natural calamities. When renewed during new harvest excess grain was likely used for export in this port(?) city.**

The King's advisors are respected for their equipoise, equilibrium, level-headedness, and the people respected the emergency plan that devised the grain storage for emergency use by the city carers [guardians (of Kozi uur)]

1110  **= thava sa ma tha La thava N Na(l) = Respected even minded revered leader. `1`When we read the Dholavera sign board, this is the background of the advisors (=thvam thar = thavaththar = thavasis) that earns them the reverence.**

Seal 6: 2056 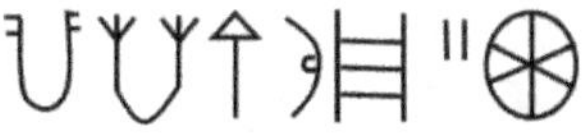 **= thava Na da na yyaa (aa) = Great Dancing Lord('s cow) = "Great Dancing Lord('s cow)**

The reason for the last sign being shown in bracket is this: the nascent state of development, the *script* has not developed all modifiers needed to sound all 216 syllables being spoken in their spoken version. Here we see the last sign being interpreted in two ways, one as cow and another as a modifier to the previous sign, sounding it long. Both are agreeable in reading but the seal reading as the Great Dancing Lord is a better fit. 'His cow' is also meaningful as Indus Tamils donated cows, as seen

elsewhere, for the benefit of the temples. 'Great Dancing Lord' as *imprint* was handed to worshipers as we see elsewhere.

Seal 7: 2068 ⚹⋃⟨⋉⟩⋋" ◇⋊ = Incomparable Tamil Mother's (temple) cows.

In reading this seal we arrive at the conclusion that the Indus-Harappan script was Tamil and the people were Tamils who worshipped Tamil Mother as a deity in a temple and cows were donated for the ongoing benefit of the temple. Seal's last sign is *ka* or *ik*, which implies plural suffix in this developing writing system. We see similar usage throughout the seals studied. More discussions follow in the article titled Tamil Grammar in Indus writings.

Conclusions: Of the many seals we studied regarding the worship practices of Tamils of the Indus-Harappan civilization, we studied few samples in this article. The study clearly shows that they worshipped many deities having links to today's worship practices of Tamils throughout the world. There are seals showing female deity, Innana (a Sumerian Goddess of war and love). This represents KoRRavai of Tamils, a war Goddess worshipped along with Siva and Lord of the Mountain. When worship was offered to Siva, the male form, therer are seals equally revering the female form as 'AaRRal aththaL'. (seal M 1181 A). You can read all the details in the cited research paper referenced earlier.

*****

Article 6: Sembian Kandiyur Stone Axe

Stone axe accidentally discovered in Tamil Nadu with Indus-Harappan inscriptions on it.

ASI Seals: 1232, 8055, 1022, 1129, 1098, 9811

Seal 1: 1232 Overseer's cow
Seal 2: 8055 Order related to temple
Seal 3: 1022 Cow related to the great temple
Seal 4: 1129: Carer of three cows of Siva
Seal 5: 1098 Respected young leader's cow
Seal 6: 9811 Aromatic ghee

This article is a focused enlargement of a few of the Indus-Harappan seals studied and published in the full research paper mentioned. The readings of seals as a language explain some aspects of this ancient multifaceted civilization both as language and civilization.

In this article we study a stone axe that was accidentally discovered by Mr. V.Shanmuganathan in Sembian Kandiyur, in TamilNadu, India, bearing inscriptions resembling the Indus-Harappan script. Here we read that inscription as Indus-Harappan signs comparing them to the signs and seals studied in the research.

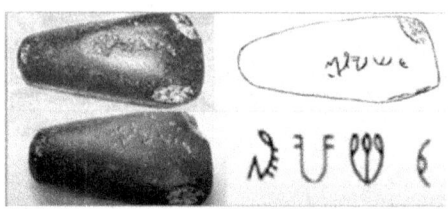

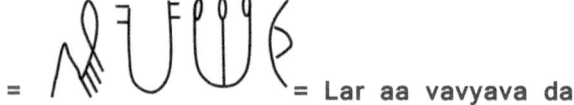

= Lar aa vavyava da

This reading by Mr. I. Mahadeven shows an obvious deviation from what is seen in the photograph (unknown credit). The sounds of the signs are: respected person, cow, related to, da(possessive).

Since this author has no access to the artifact, the study looks to the Indus seals studied for specific meaning (sounds) of the signs seen on the stone tool.

The second sign is the familiar sound 'aa' an one letter word in Tamil, meaning cow(s). This reading of the stone tool comes under question as the tool was in use and the meaning of cow does not fit.

The third sign is read by Mr.I. Mahadevan as 'vavyava' and is in conflict with what is seen in the photograph as interpreted by an unspecified reader (could be Mr. I. Mahadevan). If the

© V.P. (Ponmuthu) Shanmugham

photographic interpretation is valid, we have to reinterpret this sign to 'yya' a very close sign in appearance, the meaning closely aligning with the previous sign in the tool reading.

∪ = aa = cow

∪ = yya = respected leader

The third sign as shown in the photograph can only be read as ;ya' and not 'vavyava' as read by Mr.I. Mahadevan.

∪ = ya

) = da

∪ = vavyava [see the relationship to a pictogram of a bat]

Below we analyze the related Indus-Harappan seals to arrive at the meaning this research derives for the signs we see in the ancient stone tool.

1232 ∪ ◇ = mee mee Laar aa

Here the meaning *Lar* is 'well respected' (one's cow.)

8055 ∃∪∪△ = kooyil vavyava aa Na

Here we read the meaning of the middle two signs seen in the stone tool. 'koil related law'.

1022 ∪∪△‖◇ = mee mee koyil vavyava aa

Highly regarded koil related cow.

1098 ꓕꓵꓵꭕ ‖◇ = mee mee iLa yya aa

Well respected young leader's cow.

9811 Ψ‖‖‖"ΨꓴꙄꙄ = kama kama vyay " nay

'Very Aromatic ghee'

The research accepts the reading of two of the four signs in the axe as read by the earlier researcher, but modifies the middle two signs as different for reasons discussed. The researched reading fits well with the maanings we see in the analysis of researched Indus-Harappan seals, meaning the Stone tool belongs to a respected leader, including the Tamil grammar involved.

This brief analysis demonstrates that any and all signs found by archeological efforts in the greater Tamil Region can be read or interpreted with the understading this research developed by studying the Indus-Harappan signs and seals.

5119 ⊞ꓱꓴ)‖‖ = mu da aa thozu. In this reading there is an underlying grammar that provides a possessive. The meaning is the cowshed of the aged cow(s). This is the same meaning arrived at by the rereading of the script on the stone tool:

Researcher Mr. I. Mahadevan's:

This reads as *'Lar aa vavyava da'* = Respected one, cow, related to, da?

This researcher's reading is:

© V.P. (Ponmuthu) Shanmugham

The modified interpretation as analyzed reads as: *Lar yyaa ya da* = Respected leader's possession, which fits well with the stone tool.

$\text{\AA Y U U }$ = Lar yya ya da = Respected one's, the meaning is this stone tool 'belongs to the respected one, the leader.

This reading fits well even as we read potsherds (Egypt excavations) and gold ingots (at Theni near Madurai, in Tamil Nadu, the inscriptions in Tamizi script) showing names of people to whom they belong.

Conclusions:

When we read the Indus-Harappan script as a language, namely Tamil, we gain insights into the script found on the Sembian Kandiyur, Tamil Nadu, stone axe discovered by a Mr. V. Shanmuganathan, and read by Mr. Iravatham Mahadevan. Knowing the sounding of Indus-Harappan signs and seals in our study, we infer that the stone axe script was incorrectly interpreted in form that led to the misfitting reading (translation?).

If we slightly change one sign in the used stone axe script and accept another sign in the axe as shown handwritten in the photograph, we arrive at a reading and meaning that fits with Indus-Harappan script and archeological discoveries far and wide, with Tamizi scripts and grammar also verifying Indus-Tamizi-Tamil connections.

This analysis demonstrates that we can interpret or read the field discovered scripts in greater Tamil Nadu that show fidelity to the Indus-Harappan script as in "INDUS SIGNS and GRAFFITI MARKS of Tamil Nadu- BY Government of Tamil Nadu, Department of Archaeology". No ISBN given.

*****

Article 7: Sound modifiers

The research tool, similar to the *Rosetta Stone* that helped to read Egyptian Hieroglyphs, was developed by the late researcher Mr. Purnachandra Jeeva, to *explain* Indus-Harappan, Tamizi, and Tamil scripts. It was revised and enhanced by this author to clarify its use.

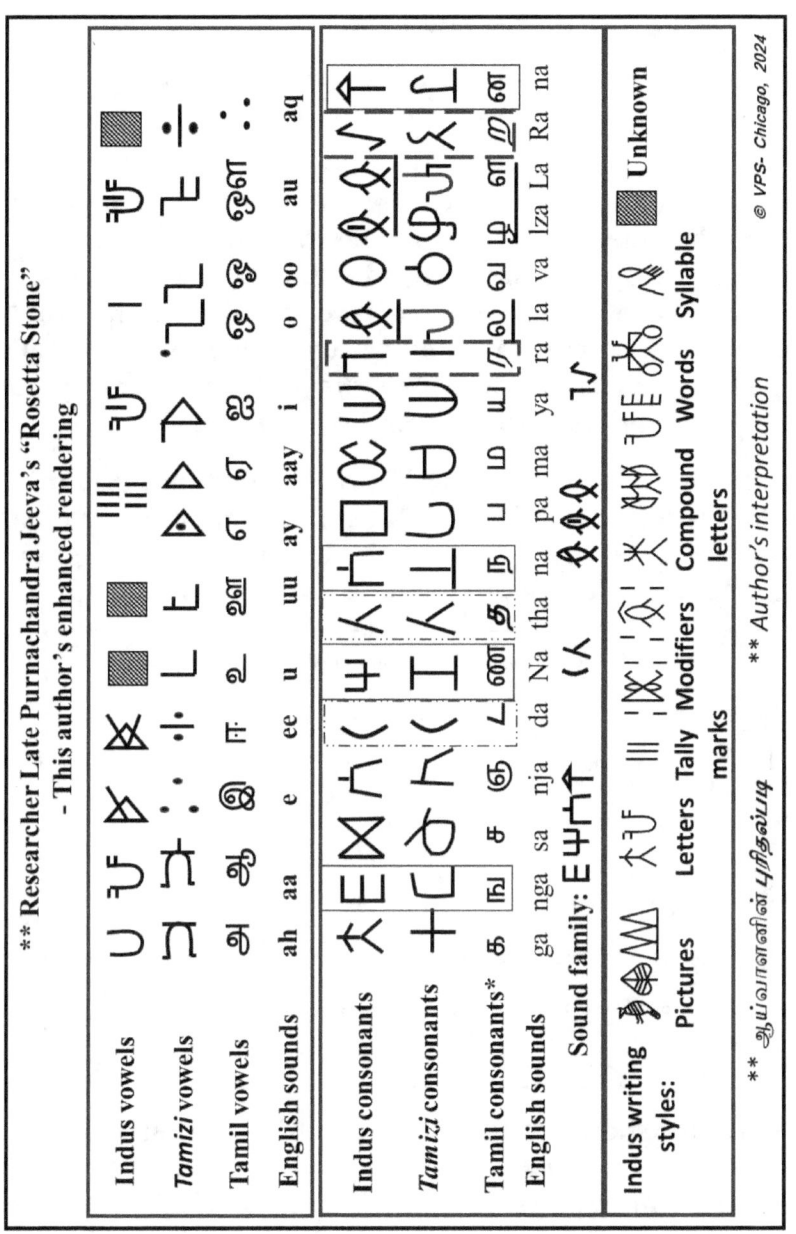

In this paper we dive deeper into the seven Indus writing styles;

Indus writing styles:							
Pictures		Letters	Tally marks	Modifiers	Compound letters	Words	Syllable

In his research work "Indus-Harappan script is a Language" this researcher identified *seven writing styles* **used as shown in this picture. Pictograms are easily identifiable and the research paper discusses how and why these were used even as the people were developing a robust writing system to express their fully developed spoken language which the research identified as Ancient Tamil understandable even by today's Tamil speakers.**

Pictograms were used for a specific reason of Tamil grammar. As seen in the tool, Indus Scribes did not *separate* **short and long 'u', two vowel sounds that made the use of Pictograms necessary, as a work-around, to sound the two vowels.**

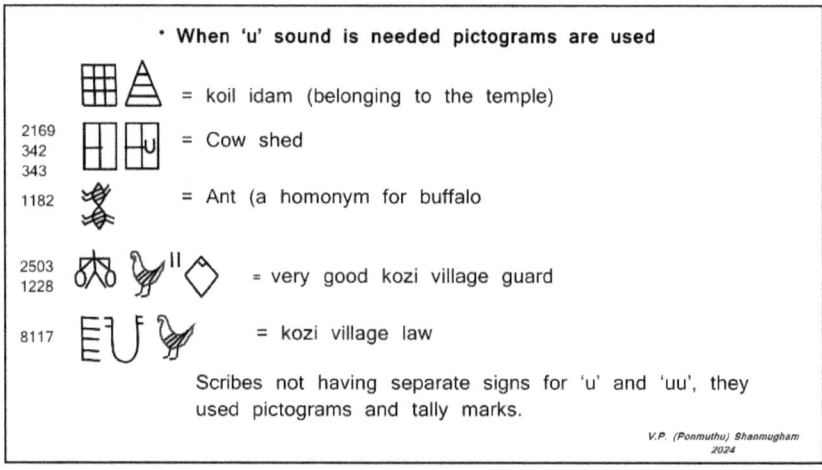

In all the seals, shown, when read as Tamil, the short and long 'u' sounds *manifest. Temple place, cowshed, ant* **– a homonym of buffalo,** *Kozi village, Prevailing ordinance of Kozi village* **are examples in Tamil.**

© V.P. (Ponmuthu) Shanmugham

More examples follow:

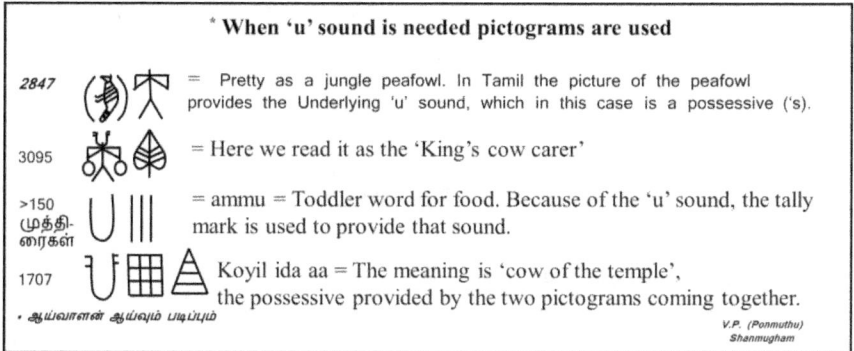

In the above seals the same pattern continues. Pretty as the peafowl of the forest, the Carer of King's cow(s), Toddler food / milk, Temple cow are readings in Tamil.

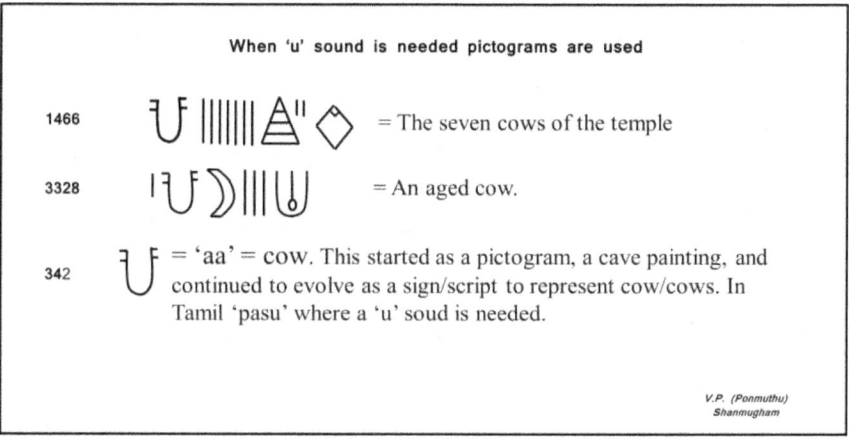

Here we also see number tally marks along with pictures that serve the same purpose of the Tamil grammar to bring out the long-short 'u' sounds. The readings are seven cows of the great temple, an aged cow, and cow.

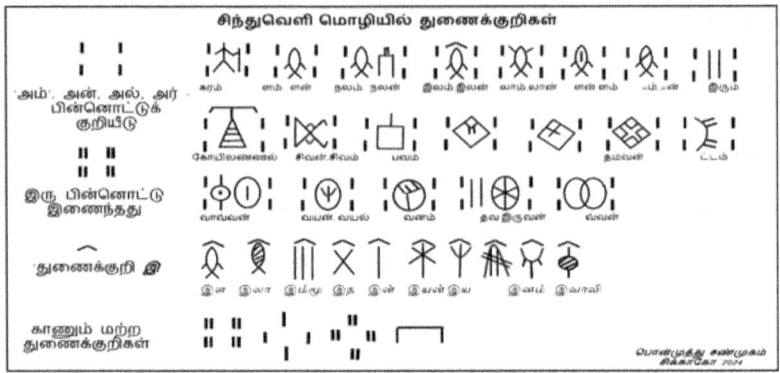

In the above picture are shown single letters (some are syllables) we see in the study. There are family of letters (sounds) that readily substitute for each other as the research shows and not all the scribes were consistent in their grammatical usage but correct within guidelines seen.

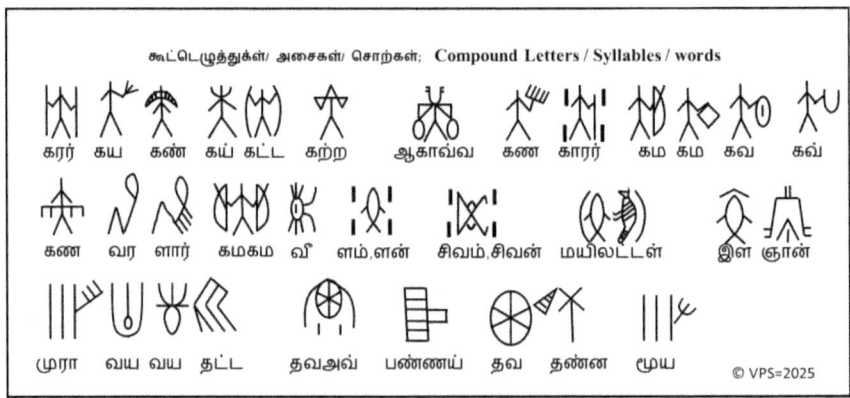

In these pictures we see individual letters, and compound letters all showing modifiers of varying shapes. In this article we take up the use of modifiers and how they evolved within the Indus-Harappan Script and how they developed subsequently in Tamizi and Tamil scripts.

Why modifiers? A basic idea of the Indus-Harappan scribe as research shows was to keep the vowels and consonants as the same in written form and use modifiers, to create syllables when each vowel conjugates with each consonant. In the following draft we see the beginnings of the list made by the Indus-Harappan script.

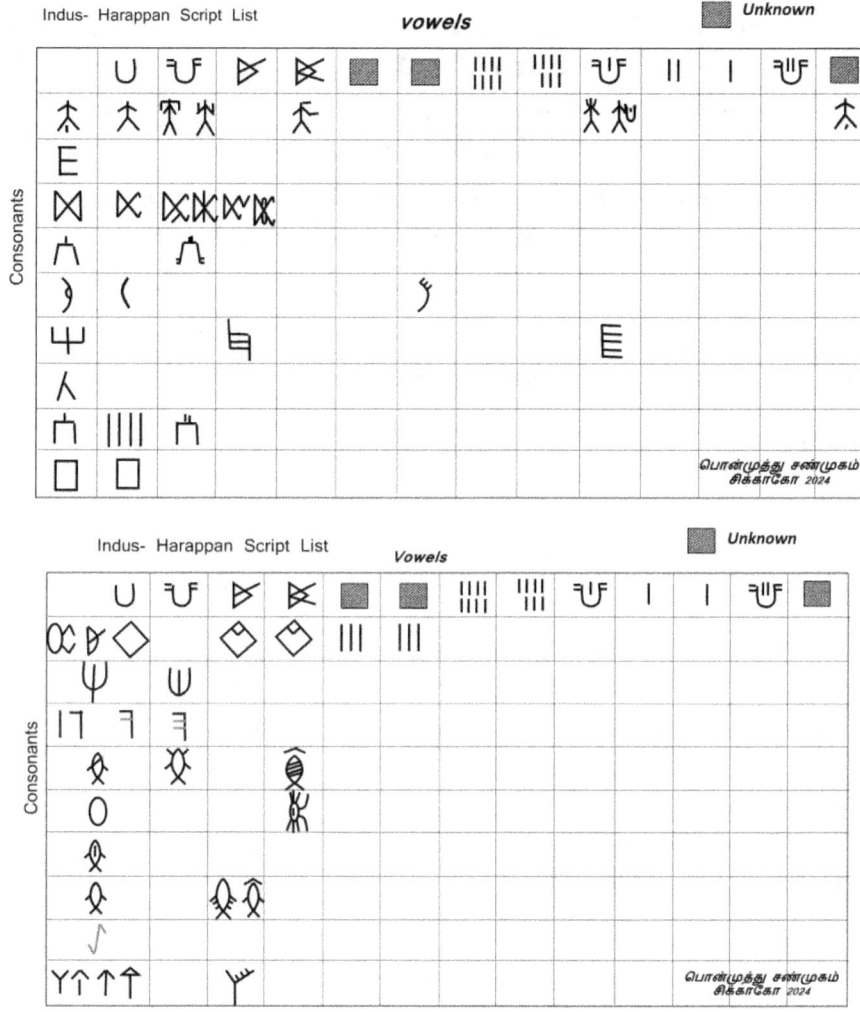

These two lists show vowels, consonants, and some syllables known to the Indus people and these lists are incomplete.

Research shows that of the 12 vowels of Tamil, two were not developed by the Indus-Harappan scribes and one was implied in use but not listed. The unknown vowels are short and long 'u' and the implied one was ஃ, which indicates all consonants. The sparsely populated tables (shown for understanding only) indicate the people's attempt to create all syllables (conjugates). They continued to experiment with modifiers, pictograms, tally marks and creating compound letters, all the while sounding them 'correctly' in their spoken form as the development shows.

Combined letters are many. Of the 400+ signs identified by the ASI Concordance many of them are such combinations.

Examples are:

🜨 🜨 = (க+ய்); ka+iy = kaiy; ka+ai = kai

𝕏 𝕏 = (ச+இ); si, si

◇ = me = respected

⚘ = aa gaa vva = cow carer (five letters combined)

𝕏 = (க+ய்); kaiy, kaya

𝕏 = (க+ண்); kaN, KaNNa

𝕏 = (க+ம); ka ma

𝕏 = (ம+க+ம); ma ka ma, kama (kama kama)

Studying individual modifiers:

This shown modifier adds one or more of the suffixes. It conveys in Tamil – *am, an, al, ar* as read. Below we see letter 'si' (itself as sa + e) get modified:

= Letter *'si'* modified by *am,* and *an,* yielding *Sivam* and *Sivan.* Two other modifiers *al* and *ar* (அல், அர்) are not meaningful here. This type of usage continues to be seen throughout the study of the Indus-Harappan script as shown in the full research paper

This compound sign reads in Tamil as *'va ya'* meaning 'strong', and this word usage is widely found in ancient Tamil literature.

When the above modifier is added to this – the reading *'va ya'* takes on one of four suffixes *(am, an, al, ar)* and reads as *'vayal'* (one that fits) – meaning the *cultivated field* in Indus script as *also* in today's Tamil.

Here we see a pictogram and a letter combination modified by the modifier we are studying. The resulting sound is *'koyil N al'* (picture is koil (temple), N letter, *al* being one of the four suffixes given by the modifier). Modifier *'an'* will also fit as *'koyil N an'.* According to prevailing Tamil grammar the N will double to provide the soundings: *koyil aNNal, Koyil aNNan,* both meaning the *Temple Leader.* This fits well with other reading of seals related to temple, its function, and role of seals related to temple etc.

This compound letter with the modifier reads as *kar ar* = *kaarar,* the *ka* taking on the long sound as Indus script does not differentiate well between long and short sounds. Here the long sound fits with the *'ar'* suffix provided by the modifier, reading the same as ⋈ , ka ar ar.

In the shown examples, we can see all four suffixes (am, an, al, ar) come out when the modifier is used, validating the Tamil grammar we hypothesized. The last example has another significance. The syllable is used with *ghee* as 'ghee seller' at Indus Valley, and the name is found in Tamil Nadu as village names: 'Ghee seller Village' showing connections! [neyk karap patti]. Ghee vendor's cry: "neyyo neyyi, kamakama neyyi!" ["நெய்யோ நெய்யி! கமகம நெய்யி!"]

The following modifier is doubled in script as the previous one:

‖ ‖

‖ ‖ The previously studied modifier gets doubled as shown, any two of four suffixes may be combined to sound the letter or syllable. Any one of *'am, an, al, ar'* can combine with any of the second set of *'am, an, al, ar'* to create the syllable containing the letter or syllable inside the modifier.

‖◌‖
‖◌‖ Here *'ma'* ◌, is combined with any combinations of the four suffixes denoted by the earlier modifier ı ı. The fitting one are more likely (ma+an+an) mannan, (ma+an+ar) mannar, (ma+al+an) mallan, (ma+al+ar) mallar, etc.

One other frequently seen modifier is ⌃, that gives 'e' sound, to the modifying letter or syllable. Modifiers are not listed separately in the concordance and no numbers assigned, true to their nature. They have names but no sound, syllabic, values.

⩍, ⩍, ⌃, ⌃ = Single letters modify and read as *ela, etha, eya, era.* You can read them in seals and verify. You can trace this modifier moving to Tamizi and to Tamil syllables, where consonants combine with the vowel 'e'. This modifier in Tamil is named 'mael vilangku' where the sounding starts with the letter - li, thi, yi, ri (லி/ளி, தி, யி, ரி).

We also see other modifiers that give a letter, the long sound. This is done in one of two ways and both look experimental by the Indus-Harappan scribe and not used with consistency.

For example, the *ka* sound is made long *kaa* sound by this modifier ⌐⌐.

1⼤ + ⌐⌐ = 10 ⼤ Short *ka* sound modified by the modifier shown to sound long *kaa* sound. Is it a coincidence that this modifier keeping almost the same shape becomes ⊓ in Tamil which makes all short '*a*' syllable into long '*aa*' sounds with no form change (வரிவடிவம்) to the letter involved? Also, this modifier like all others does not have a sound value by itself, only a name.

Another unique modifier used by the Indus-Harappan scribe is using the long *aa letter* ∪, as a modifier in some places.

⼤∪ⓘ◯∪ In seal 3246 these are the five signs that get combined into one compound letter by a scribe who finds efficiency because of the very limited space of a seal. As written, the second letter from left is used as a modifier, sounding the short '*ka*' into long '*kaa*' sound [⼤]. We see the first four signs (letters) combined as ⼤◯, read as *kaavva* and the fifth '*aa*' sign added on the top to keep it the same sign ∪, the newly created complex but efficient sign reading as a word ⼤◯ '*aakaavva*' a *cow carer*. A tally mark next to this word, indicates how many cows the bearer of the seal/imprint can care for, both as responsibility and for proper compensation. There are many such seals of this type seen like, 𑀔𑀺𑀥|||, carer of three cows.

We also see two modifiers combining to enhance sounds creating a word, a word that is still in use in today's Tamil.

𑀑𑀺 In this sign we see two of the modifiers we studied so far. The letter getting modified is the '*l*' sound. First modifier make it sound '*i-l*', and the second modifier adds the '*am*' suffix (most fitting of the four) making the word sound '*illam*' where, by archeologically verified Tamil grammar, the middle sound doubles. The sound is '*illam*' meaning 'home', and this appears in few seals, as '*world is a big home*', '*home of the elder and alone*' *etc.*

Similarly sign 61 𑀔𑀺𑀟 reads as '*nalam* or *nalan* (நலம் / நலன்)

These appearance and development of modifiers continue in Tamizi with more consistency and an attempt to keep all letters with minimal change with some degree of success as the research of Tamizi shows. However, almost all conflicts and imperfections are removed in Tamil script though we see some remnants of difficulty encountered by the Indus scribes and Tamizi scribes, most of which is in rock-cut inscriptions, and scribing (*NOT writing*) on palm leaves.

In the Thamizi list we can see the modifiers trying to provide consistency across all the 216 syllables of 18 consonants, showing the same structure as Tamil. In some places letters do not keep their shape as they take on more than one modifier (modifier over modifier) showing some difficulty to identify the letter. These are almost rectified in Tamil where all 216 syllables clearly show the letter form irrespective of the one or many modifiers used. Tamil does have instances where a modifier is modified by another modifier to create syllables, indicating its ancient *Tamizi* connection. Also, Tamizi uses only three or four modifiers in 21 arrangements to sound all 216 syllables.

Conclusions:

On this topic of modifiers, we studied many of the sound modifiers used by the Indus-Harappan scribes. These modifiers modify letters or syllabic sounds trying to keep the 'letter' script without change. In the nascent state of development of writing the people who were speaking an already well-developed language and in use, show many attempts to use modifiers consistently keeping the form of the letter constant. However, they did not carry this design throughout the writing system and created *pictograms, tally marks, and compound letters and syllables* as a work around. We can see this modifier design mature in *Thamizi* scripts where more of the design objective of the Indus-Harappan scribes has been achieved with yet some room for improvement. These deficiencies are again corrected in Tamil script with a hint of this connection with *Tamizi* remaining where *a modifier modifies another modifier* to create a syllable, generally not acceptable Tamil grammar!

*****

Article 8: Uses of Seals

Research of the Indus-Harappan Seals over the past 100 years has not yielded a key aspect of how the seals were used. Of the over 4000 seals found as artifacts, we read some of them to demonstrate how these short expressions were used in the day-to-day life of the people.

Here, as examples, we see tally marks denoting numbers from one to five, and followed by few letters:

Tally marks as numbered in ASI concordance

Signs: I , II , III , IIII , IIIII

| 86 | 87 | 89 | 95 | 96 |

Below are examples of some signs as in the ASI Concordance

© V.P. (Ponmuthu) Shanmugham

人 1 = ka

人 + $\sqcap$ = 木 10 = kaa [the second mark does not appear separately, only combined]

U 342 = aa

O 373 = va

$\uparrow$ 211 = n, na

The above five individual signs (Tamil letters, modifier) combine to create compound words

木 + O + O = ᘒ 12 = kaa v va = guarding, guard, care

ᘒ + $\uparrow$ = ᘒ 14 = kaa v va n = male carer

U + ᘒ = ᘒ 15 = aa kaa v va = ஆ கா வ் வ = cow care(r)

Combining the tally marks with these words we see many seals used in the study.

Seal 2343 ᘒ | | | | = four aa gaa v va = Carer of four cows.

2472 ᘒ U 🌿 = Male carer of King's cows

There are numerous seals similar to this with variations in the tally marks. The readings are: carer of one *cow*, carer of two *cows* etc.

These seal imprints are made of baked clay for longevity, implying manner of usage. In the agrarian society cows provide many benefits and they were taken care of by dedicated carers. The tally marks tell us how many cows a carer is invested with caring, based on his skills and experience, and this also must have accounted in his compensation.

With this analysis, we conclude that those who cared for the cows carried these seals as a permit or authorization. We can extend these activities or duties of the carers in addition to grazing the animals, housing them in sheds, providing fodder and water for them, caring for the un-weaned calves, milking producing cows and the sanitation of the cow sheds. In this analysis we see one of the uses of the seals – many seals validating this reading.

In a similar approach in the broader research as shown in the research referenced, we study individual signs as ancient Tamil and interpret the seals to demonstrate the various uses of the seals.

When milk is produced at a cow shed for instance, it is distributed to cow owners and others who may not own producing cows:

1326 ⽥⦀⦀U⛎⛎" ◇ = mee mee la iLa(m) vya muu n = very good fresh milk (vyamun = milk) [study of 40+ seals yield this understanding]

Here we have a seal declaring quality fresh milk. Being a seal, scribed from right to left, it reads from left to right '*correctly*', when IMPRINTED on to wet clay. What purpose did the imprint serve?

Just expressed milk is shared with owners of cows, and the rest is shared with those who do not own producing cows. Here we see the above seal come in to play.

Those who want to distribute fresh milk, obtained this authorization from leaders of the community, farmers guild, etc. providing sufficient information as to their process that assures safety and quality of milk. Therefore, this seal from the authorizing authority creates IMPRINTS to whomever wants to setup distribution of fresh milk, meeting and assuring existing guidelines, ordinances of the village or city. A seal imprint is so small to see and read and so necessarily the need exists to create a large banner or notice board on materials like cloth, wood planks, etc. to inform the public. This again *implies* the high literacy rate of the population and these skills were not the exclusive right of the leaders and the 'powerful' elite as is interpreted in other civilizations! Not all banners can be pictograms! We see a signboard at Dolavira we studied earlier to prove the point.

2648 ⊞Ψ||||"◇ = mee na y thozu = very good ghee shed

This seal declares a very good ghee shed in the village / city. The approval to operate this shed came from authority via the imprint of this seal, again demonstrating the one use of the seal.

Taking a deeper dive, we need to answer a question as to why a separate shed for Ghee? If we combine the seals we studied so far, we can deduce that fresh milk is valuable but naturally degrades in quality over time, and that needs to be addressed. So, we see ordinances that *imply* time-controlled distribution of milk.

5274 line 1: ℲՍ𝖉⊞⊞ = ida ma aa N(ay) = Prevailing ordinance / law of this place (village / city)

We may not know what this ordinance was in detail but it certainly covered the safety and wellbeing of the people of the place. When we see fresh milk being distributed with authorization, the authority needs to provide in the laws, for the degrading of the milk over certain period. So, this ordinance might well be covering the duration of distribution of fresh milk beyond which the aging milk *before spoilage* should be sent to the Ghee Shed for conversion to stable useful products like curd, buttermilk, butter and ghee, which were again made available to the people as some seals we studied verify.

Since we see seals in all these categories, interpretation of the previous seals as Tamil language and their usage is validated.

3015 ⵟⵊⵊⵁⵁⵁⵁⵁ di di ay laa iLa vyamuun = just expressed fresh milk [di di = thideer (திடீர்); aylaa (similar to ailasaa in boating) = milking (repeat movement)

The imprint of this seal permits the bearer to set up distribution of fresh milk, meeting quality standards.

2617 ⵊⵊⵁ = ivva da d l vya muu r muraa = Here available buttermilk

The imprint of this seal permits the bearer to set up distribution of buttermilk.

9811 ⵁⵊⵊⵁ = makama (kamakama) vya ya "na y" = aromatic ghee

Here the imprint of the seal declares aromatic ghee.

1427 ⵁⵊⵊⵁ = y na kar = nay kar = Ghee 'seller'

Bearer of the imprint of this seal can distribute ghee.

1447 ⵁⵁⵁⵁ = ma laa La saa Na(m) = Heaped manure (available) [offer by cattle shed]

Here the imprint of this seal announces (by a cow shed?) heaped manure as available (*necessarily in a banner*).

4371 ⋿∪⟩⊨⚹⚹⟭ = ma laa La paNNa da aa N(ai) = Order of the Farmers Guild

This seal declared the order arrived at by the Farmers Guild, the details most likely provided by some means which may not have survived the ravages of time.

We also see some seals that provide proof of ownership:

4084 ∪⚹⚹∪∪⟩||| = muu da av ay laa kay aa = the elder lady's hand-raised cow.

This seal identifies a cow as belonging to an elder lady as we see seals identifying cows belonging to the king and others.

2472 ⊗∪✿ = arasa aa kaavvan = Carer of King's [✿] cows

Since city ordinances, regulations require cowsheds to be outside city limits (various laws we see but do not know exactly the details) we have to conclude that this lady, seal 4084, kept her cow in one of the commercial cowsheds, most likely a shed that houses and cares for producing cows. We also see other sheds for oxen, for older animals, etc.

1387 ◈∪⚹⇡⊞ = mee thava da la n thozu = mee thava thaLan thozu = Cowshed of Thavathalan (proper name) [An imprint]

Coupled with seal 4084 above, we infer that the elder lady surrendered her cow and calf to the care of a shed like this one which cared for them and she received daily share of milk. The

proof of her ownership of the animals and service benefits are assured with a seal like the one shown, which is to be verified as metal or baked clay, for longevity. It could be metal by the fact that the script of the seal is readable from left to right. If it is of metal the way to make it at that time was to use the lost-wax-casting method, which was known to the IVC Tamils from Mehrgarh days. Making wax models in volume is easy with a stone or baked clay mold (positive model). Casting with sand, clay mold may have been involved, but needs verification with field artifacts and data.

This seal could also be of baked clay as it can be made by imprinting with a stone seal and baking the 'correctly' reading imprint, for long life as the usage demands.

There are other types of seals whose imprints were distributed at temples during worship.

2234  **= vay ya iru illam = The world is a big home (declaring universal brotherhood)**

What purpose the imprints of this seal served and where etc.? This seal expresses a sentiment of a very mature civilization declaring the principle of universal brotherhood. Let us explore.

The Indus-Harappan civilization is labelled with a time of beginning and decline with whatever evidence available and whatever valid method used for its determination. But this seal's sentiment defies the calendar as to when does a civilization arrive at such a lofty ideal that will solve so many of the human problems even today?

The Tamils of the Indus-Harappan civilization were speaking their well-developed language even before the calendar defines the IVC beginnings. This is verified in the way the written script develops as detailed in the main research paper referenced and throughout our study.

We see Tamils worshipping their language as a deity in a temple in the following seal,

2068 ⟨glyphs⟩ = thami thami lzaththaL aa k(kaL) = Incomparable Tamil Mother's (temple) Cows.

Question arises as to how these Tamils worshipped Tamil Mother in a temple setting? Who was guiding them in this worship? What was being said, talked about at the worship? Just rituals?

The research tries to piece together what we know so far.

⟨glyphs⟩
ஆள்அவிஎச்ச

2420   This is a well-known seal, imprinted, and the script read by late researcher Jeeva as shown, meaning 'Compassionate Siva'. How was this imprint used? Presumably used in worship at a temple for Siva. Clay imprints on wet clay were given out to worshippers after service to remember!

We have another sign/seal that can show who was leading the worship at such temples.

207 ⟨glyph⟩ = koyil N al/an = koyilaNNal/an. Spearhead / lead at the Temple.

This sign specifies a lead at various temples in whatever way the Indus-Harappan Tamils worshipped various deities we see. One possible use for the seal above (2420) was to imprint it and provide the clay imprints to worshippers after the Temple Lead most likely elaborated the age accumulated wisdom of *their Tamil ancients*.

There are many seals describing various deities like Siva, Bull faced Lord, Lord with Third Eye of Wisdom, Lord of the

Mountain, Dancing Lord, my able leader, etc., described in the main research paper.

In the same way, when the Tamils worshipped at Tamil Mother's Temple, there was elaboration of her past glory and the knowledge gained by forefathers, being passed on to their descendants as memory literature. One such wisdom is the seal 2234, The world is a big home! This seal imprint on wet clay was distributed to all worshippers to remember the ancient wisdom to *guide their daily living*. This can explain few things.

-Wisdom like this was passed on from generation to generation by word of mouth for a long time as *memory literature*, before the attempt to put them in writing
-This fabled past is the possible (First) Tamil Academy seen in ancient Tamil Literature and the Indus Civilization is during the Second Tamil Academy when writing was being developed (not as the seat of second academy)
-Wisdom like this kept the Indus-Harappan people strong from within and the need for governance was kept to a minimum by enlightened leadership
-The fact that this civilization lived in relative peace for a very long time (unless we find evidences to the contrary) indicates the strength of character that develops from within, a hallmark of Tamil lineage much elaborated in their 'ARam' literature
-All references to guard, village guards etc. - show different meanings – guarding (=caring for) cows, guarding the cultivated fields, guarding the people from natural calamities, like flood, fire, crop failure, etc.

-The idea of granary indicates that the saved grain was a buffer in times of urgent need as described and when renewed with new harvest, the surplus grain was used in overseas commerce. This idea is entirely different from prevailing ideas of granaries in a slavery-based ancient civilization, like that of the Egyptian or even the *recent* medieval period of feudalism of Europe and elsewhere in recent history.

1110 (Script from RMRL Web Tool) ΕΕ⊕ჯ⋀ᲪᲙ⊕=
thava sa ma tha la thava N N = thava samathala thavaNNa(l) =
A great equipoised respected Leader

As we read such seals as this, which describes a leader of equanimity, we can easily see the consequences of such leadership. Weather this describes leaders in the community, advisors (Thavasis) to the king or the King himself [Tholavira(n) – one who never lose a battle]. Such a leader necessarily has conquered himself (from his own desires and passions) to be unconquerable! All this indicate the presence of 'yoga' practices in this Ancient Tamil Civilization which is also verifiable by the yogic postures we see in few seals.

Conclusions

From this brief treatise we can understand some of the ways the Indus-Harappan seals were used by the people. We can summarize some of the uses:

-Authorized approvals for
  Setting up and offering services
  Make products for public use
  Distribute products
  Deliver services and receive benefits
  Ownership document
  Receipts
  Record events as History (covered in the main study)
  Received at Temple worship services
  Seal imprints of wisdom
  Temple related donations
  Orders, ordinances, commands, dictates related to governance
  Seals used in commerce (not covered in this study)
    (Yet to be found uses)

*****

Article 9: Tamil Grammar in Indus Script

Few articles in this series examined some Indus-Harappan seals and established that the language of the Indus-Harappan people, both spoken and written, was ancient Tamil. The research also established that the spoken language was much older and the study demonstrated that the effort to create a written script was evolving at the Indus Valley proving this point.

Here we examine some aspects of Tamil grammar that is seen and how this shows up in the writing of the Indus-Harappan script even as it was evolving.

Singular and plural indicators:

In Tamil grammar the singular and plural suffixes are shown at the end of a word. The developing Indus-Harappan script shows this evolution of indicating suffix in some seals.

© V.P. (Ponmuthu) Shanmugham

This compound sign is a word that combined five signs, though one of them (third one below), a modifier indicating a long sound, does not appear separately in the ASI concordance but shown integrated with sign 1, as sign number 10, 木. A modifier has only name and has no sound value.

U + 木 + ⌐ + O + O = 木 = aa ka aa v va = cow carer
342 1   373   15

This seal does not specify the gender of the one caring for the cow. We see in another sign, 211, that reads as 'in' (இன் – Tamil). When this combines with the above compound word, we have the following:

342 12 211 342 14

U + 木 + ↑ = U 木 = aa kaavva n = male cow carer

Here we see the suffix indicating a gender is used. This usage of gender indicating suffix is verifiably seen in many seals.

1045 木 (Ѱ) 387 = vaya kaavvan = vayal (also valiya) kaavvan = a male guard of the cultivated field (guarding watering needs, from wild animals?)

2169 ⊞↑↑⍭⋒⎅U = a ma aar da na n thozu = amayarthanan (proper name) thozu. In this name of a shed (the pictogram) we see the suffix coming at the end of the proper name of the owner, indicating gender, male.

1551 ↑ ⵊ || '' ◇ = mee mee iru La n

The seal is a name of Highly Regarded 'IruLan', name of a deity (or a so named person), the suffix showing the gender, male.

In Tamil grammar the female gender indicating suffix is 'iL' (எ in Tamil), and this we see in seal number 2068,

2068 〼 = thami tami lzaththaL aa kka(L) = Incomparable Tamil Mother's (temple) Cows.

In this seal the 'Tamilz aththa<u>L</u>' has the suffix 'iL' (எ Tamil) indicating the deity is female, as Mother Tamil. The male deities are addressed as 'aththan' (அத்தன் Tamil), widely seen in Tamil literature old and new with the suffix n (ன்) indicating a male. A unique seal below gives us a challenge!

M1181A 〼 = aa RRa la th tha = powerful lord (male, female). The script reads in Tamil *implying* a suffix as shown - aththan, indicating a male deity, widely seen in Tamil literature. The suffix added can be feminine as aththaL, as some interpret the figure as female, matching matriarchy arguments, and the practice of 'yoga' is common to both genders. This seal supports both readings. Credit: Asko Parpola et all, Helsinki.

〼(64), 〼(63) = mayil (a)tta L (one is a seal, the other is an imprint) = pretty as a peafowl.

This compound (pictogram and letter) sign describes a deity of war as a female with the suffix 'iL' (எ in Tamil) shown by the sign 59 *'inside'*. [sign numbers as in ASI Catalogue]

Also, we have a suffix 'ay' ('ஐ' Tamil) that indicates female gender.

4084 ∪ ⵊⵙ ∪ ⑂)||| = muu da av ay laa kai aa = Hand-raised cow of the Elder Lady

In this reading of the seal the owner of the cow is shown as *'av ay'*, *av* meaning one filled with (beauty, knowledge, wisdom, *and* age - in popular use) and the *ay* indicating gender. The male gender receives the suffix 'en' (ஐயன்) as we saw earlier in other seals. Avvar/n is also acceptable male version and appears in some seals.

Another Tamil grammar involves the suffix that indicates singular and plural. The letter below, which started out as a pictogram during cave paintings, represented cow.

. ∪ 342 = aa = cow (face of a cow, two horns, two ears)

Here, this one letter word can be both singular and plural. In the Indus-Harappan script, it starts out without specifying any suffix and implying plural in many places. The same letter is also used as a modifier to create long sounds from their short version (Grammar: குறில், நெடில்).

2343 ⊘⋀⊘|||| = four aa gaa v va = Carer of four cow<u>s</u>. In reading this seal, because of the tally mark for four, we read this as carer of four *cow<u>s</u>*, with plural suffix. But the sign in the seal does not show this suffix, only implies.

As the script evolves (spoken language is fully developed one), we see efforts to distinguish singular and plural usage of the one letter word as was in their spoken form.

3328 |∪ ⟩|||∪ = Aged (old) cow one

In scribing this seal, the scribe indicates that the cow is singular by adding the tally mark for one at the end, which is where the singular-plural suffix is normally shown in Tamil speech and writing. To differentiate from *its letter (ஒ, ஓ, இ)ர்),* form the mark is halved.

2068 ⚶ = Incomparable, peerless, Great Tamil Mother's (temple) cows

In this reading of the seal as Tamil, we see last letter 'ka' (க, க்-Tamil) standing for 'kaL' (கள் Tamil) a plural suffix in Tamil, rendering the meaning as *cows*.

In another grammar note Tamil contains many a consonant that doubles in usage. This practice was absent or only implied for a long time in rock cut inscriptions, and scribing (NOT writing) on palm leaves and even in Tamizi graffiti marks on potsherds - Potsherd found in Egypt (port of Quseir of Quadim) by Don S. Whitcomb, Janet H. Johnson 1982, Oriental Institute, University of Chicago. This author's rendering of *Thamizi* scripts seen in the photos:

＋Ⅰ ℒ = ka N n = kaNNan

ʃ 𝝀 ℒ = sa tha n = saththan

Some of the doubling letter signs are shown in the picture below, where the *form* of *'a'* ∪ is *sometimes* used to double the sounds shown:

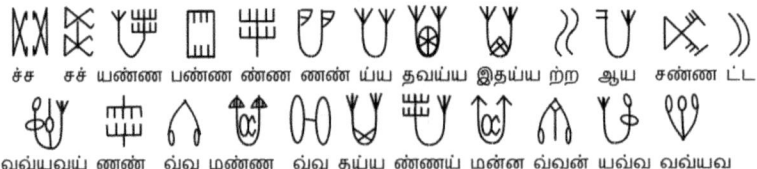

There may be other languages that evolved using Indus-Harappan script that may show this feature, but this is seen in the Indus-Harappan script that is about 5000 years before present. This brief treatise does not go into the study of all seals that contain such signs. The main research paper noted earlier contains *some* of them and some of them are seen in this series of articles.

Article 7 in this series deals in details with the *modifiers*, a great innovation in Indus-Harappan Tamil script, which started in the Indus-Harapan period and continued development in Tamizi, attaining full development in the Tamil Script of today.

Besides this brief research on Tamil Grammar, researcher Mr. Purnachandra Jeeva has written elaborately on other aspects of Tamil Grammar in the Indus-Harappan script in his (Tamil) work 'sinthuveLiyil munthu thamil' [Ancient Tamil in Indus Valley], ISBN 978-81-942791-0-5, published in 2020. This author is highlighting some new insights, not wanting to repeat earlier works.

*****

Conclusions

This collection of articles took a deeper dive into few important topics in our study of the Indus-Harappan civilization with new hypotheses. That the Indus-Harappans spoke a fully developed language for a long time before the people invented a writing system to match their spoken language. This spoken and written forms are ancient form of Tamil that is understandable even by today's Tamil speakers, 80 million in over 150 countries, nearly 5,000 years later.

We explored all of these with chosen topics and seals that well explained and provided convincing validation of the hypotheses. Whether it be the interrelationships of the seals, the people's farming activities, worships, enlightened governance, the many and varied uses of the puzzling seals, and above all, the Tamil grammar that binds so well the explored 100 or so seals together without contradictions.

The archeological research world was trying to prove everything else from varying points of view, perhaps with *inherent bias* in their research methods. Though this research has answered many unknowns, there are and will be questions that need to be raised and explored. Every seal correctly read leads to many more seals with the same *soundings* and grammar, the author estimating more than half of all existing seals. Most of these are related to the fields researched and specific vocabulary is a must to understand the rest.

Another note on the signs: this author's vocabulary is limited to his lifetime experiences in farming, animal husbandry, dealing with laws, and learned philosophy and worldview of Tamils in his growing up years, which has helped with identifying the 'basic sounds' (phonemes) of about 350 out of 400+ signs of the Indus-Harappan Script.

What is needed to complete this study is for researchers with background in pottery, weaving, metalwork, carpentry, ship building, sea voyage, etc., to come together and read the rest of the seals with given insights in this work, to arrive at the fuller picture of this ancient multifaceted first Indian Civilization. Calling it as 'Indian Civilization' itself may be erroneous, as we see their global view of human potential. The author thanks all the dedicated efforts of so many for so long in so many ways in the past that helped in this research and modestly presents this current work for the current researchers' fair review on its merit, and wish the best in the efforts by those who may yet take up this study to find answers for questions not yet answered or even raised.

Bibliography

1. Archeological Survey of India, Indus Script, Texts Concordance and Tables – By Iravatham Mahadevan 1977

2 .Corpus of Indus Seals and Inscriptions, 1. Collection in India –Jagat Pati Joshi and Asko Parpola, Helsinki, '87

3 .Corpus of Indus seals and Inscriptions, 2. Collections in Pakistan –Sayid Mustafa and Asko Parpola et all, Helsinki, '91

4 .Credit: Photographs of all the seals shown are credited to the references 2 and 3 above- Asko Parpola et. All

5 .sinthuveliyil munthu thamiz (சிந்துவெளியில் முந்து தமிழ் – written in Tamil) by Purnachandra Jeeva, yalisai pathipagam, 2020. ISBN 978 81 9427 910 5

6 .Roja Muttiah Research Library, Chennai, India. The research tool: https://indusscript.in

7. Indus Script As a Language – சிந்துவெளியின் மொழி, by V.P.(Ponmuthu) Shanmugham, Sowmi Printers, Kovai, 2026. ISBN 979-8-9940362-6-6 (Bilingual, declared as Tamil)